history bites

The Past's Strangest Moments —In Bite-size Portions

Sterling Publishing Co., Inc.
New York

JUDITH MILLIDGE

Library of Congress Cataloging-in-Publication Data Available

2 4 6 8 10 9 7 5 3 1

Published by Sterling Publishing Co., Inc.
387 Park Avenue South, New York, NY 10016
© 2005 PRC Publishing
Distributed in Canada by Sterling Publishing
c/o Canadian Manda Group, 165 Dufferin Street
Toronto, Ontario, Canada M6K 3H6
Distributed in Great Britain by Chrysalis Books Group PLC
The Chrysalis Building, Bramley Road, London W10 6SP, England

Printed in Malaysia

Sterling ISBN 1 4027 2497 7

Cover and inside image © LWA-Paul Chmielowiec/CORBIS

contents

Royal Encounters

Greek Tragedy

Philip II of Macedon was much married—he almost saw it as his duty to take up with a representative local woman of the region he was currently engaged in conquering. He married for the seventh time in October 337 BC, taking as his bride the teenaged Cleopatra, the daughter of a Macedonian aristocrat. This time, Philip said he was in love, a statement that was guaranteed to wound his queen Olympias, (the mother of Alexander the Great). At the wedding feast, Attalus the bride's uncle toasted the happy couple with the wish that the marriage would produce legitimate heirs. This remark, spoken in front of Philip's eldest son and legitimate heir, was tactless in the extreme and prompted Alexander to hurl his cup at Attalus. In turn, a drunken Philip lunged at Alexander with his sword but collapsed behind a banqueting couch, where he spent the remainder of his wedding night.

Olympias had her revenge after Philip's assassination the following year, when she forced Cleopatra to commit suicide.

Philip of Macedon was the youngest of four brothers and had spent part of his childhood in the neighboring state of Thebes as a hostage where he had studied the military reforms of his country's enemies. When he inherited the throne, he instantly improved the Macedonian army and went on to conquer great tracts of northern Greece. It was during the siege of Methone in 354 BC that he was struck by an arrow in his right eye, a life-threatening injury that he nevertheless overcame. His surgeon became famous for removing the arrow (along with the right eye) with such skill that the king's face was not left deformed. It is interesting to note, however, that all surviving coins from Philip's reign show only the left profile of his face.

When his father Philip of Macedon was presented with an apparently ungovernable horse, 12-year-old Alexander studied the beast to assess what scared it. He took the animal's head and gently turned him around so that he faced the sun and couldn't see his own shadow, which had terrified him. The horse immediately calmed down, enabling Alexander to mount him. He reined him in, then let him burn off his energy by galloping at full speed. According to Plutarch, his proud father said "O my son, look thee out a kingdom equal to and worthy of thyself, for Macedonia is too little for thee."

Alexander went on to fulfill his father's wishes, naming the horse Bucephalus because his head seemed "as broad as a bull's." Bucephalus proved to be a reliable mount, carrying Alexander across thousands of miles as he built a great empire. When he died in 326

BC in Alexander's last battle, the king did not simply bury the horse, but founded a town in his memory, Bucephela (thought to be modern-day Jhelum in Pakistan).

Caligula's Cruelty

The Roman Emperor Caligula was despotic, capricious, and dangerous, prone to executing people on a whim and enacting cruel and stupid laws. Contemporaries recognized this and struggled to cope with his increasingly lunatic orders. Convinced of his own divine status, Caligula ordered all the images of Greek gods famed either for their beauty or veneration to be brought to Rome so that he could cut off their heads and substitute his own.

He was famous for his incestuous devotion to his sisters and when his favorite sister Drusilla died, Caligula ordered public mourning, during which time, according to Suetonius, "it was capital [punishable by death] for any person to laugh, use the bath, or sup with his parents, wife, or children."

He pampered his favorite horse Incitatus with a marble stable, jeweled housings, a retinue of slaves, and held dinner parties in the horse's name. Whether or not Incitatus was created a consul is unclear.

His three-year reign of terror was ended by assassination and Suetonius reports that at first people did not believe it—they thought

Caligula himself had released the rumors to see how the populace would react.

tomb Raider

William the Conqueror invaded England in 1066 and changed the course of English history. He was a controversial figure and his actions in crushing Anglo-Saxon resistance provoked angry entries in various chronicles. His greatest administrative testament was the Domesday Book, the detailed catalogue of the English realm and distribution of the land. Ironically, William never read a single word as he couldn't actually read; all his documents and charters were signed with an X.

When William the Conqueror died on 9 September 1087 in Caen, it is said that he was so fat that his corpse could barely be crammed into the stone sarcophagus, and once in, it burst spectacularly, filling the church with a foul odor. The monkish author of the *Anglo-Saxon Chronicle* does not actually report on the funeral itself in great detail, but does remark rather waspishly:

"Alas! How false and how uncertain is this world's weal! He that was before a rich king, and lord of many lands, had not then of all his land more than a space of seven feet! And what was enshrouded in gold and gems lay there covered with mould!"

Royal encounters

hunted down

It is well known that William Rufus was killed while hunting in the New Forest, but historians are divided as to whether his death was an accident or an assassination. Rufus had received a letter from the Abbott of Gloucester warning him of danger if he left his castle, but he ignored the advice and was shot by Walter Tirrel, a man with a reputation as a crack-shot. One other person was in the New Forest on the same day: William's ambitious younger brother Henry, who inherited the crown, by-passing the claim of his elder brother Robert.

Fiery Redhead

Henry II of England (reigned 1154–1189) ruled over a large extended empire encompassing England and large parts of France. He rarely spent longer than a few months in any one place as he was occupied with defending his extensive borders. There are no contemporary portraits of him, but an excellent description survives, written by Peter of Blois in a letter to Walter, Archbishop of Palermo in 1177 which is not quite as sycophantic as many regal biographies. Henry needed some good publicity in the wake of his involvement with the murder of Thomas à Becket in 1170, and while noting Henry's many excellent characteristics, such as his care for the poor, his devotion to learning, and his love of hard work, Peter described the king's physical condition in incredible detail, from his "boxer's arms," to the "joint of his foot [where] the part of the toenail is grown into the flesh of his foot, to the vehement outrage of the whole foot."

Henry II inherited the red hair and fiery temperament of the Plantagenets, and several chroniclers attest to his quick temper when offended. In 1166, John of Salisbury wrote to Archbishop Becket that the king flew into a rage when one of his retinue spoke in favor of King William of Scotland. "And the king flying into his usual temper, flung his cap from his head, pulled off his belt, threw off his cloak and clothes, grabbed the silken coverlet of the couch, and sitting as it might be on a dung heap started chewing pieces of straw."

The kings of England and Scotland were in disagreement about various land grants in the north, but no one is really sure quite why Henry's rage was so violent on this occasion.

queen of queens

In some countries, extravagant display and glamorous clothes simply underlined the magnificence of the ruler and it was a brave courtier who wore anything that outshone the clothes of the king, queen, duke, or count. In the 14th and 15th centuries, many European merchants became wealthy as trade with the east increased and they could afford to dress in gorgeous silks and velvets. Some rulers did not appreciate these new ornaments to their courts. When the new queen of Philip the Fair arrived in Bruges in 1301 and was faced by a sea of really well-dressed subjects, she was heard to say, "I thought I was the queen, but I see there are hundreds."

SINKING EMPEROR

The Holy Roman Emperor Frederick Barbarossa (1123–1190) devoted his life to establishing his realm as pre-eminent in Europe, and to introducing Christianity in the Holy Land. In 1189 he departed for the Third Crusade, having established peace in Germany. His army was experienced, but had to travel through Turkey during the summer months "through the glare of the sun and the burning heat of summer along a tortuous road." In an effort to lessen the strain on his troops, Barbarossa made a catastrophic decision: he decided to ford the Saleph River in southeastern Turkey while wearing full armor. The contemporary chronicler recorded somewhat wryly, "Wise though he was in other ways, the Emperor foolishly tried his strength against the current and plunged into a whirlpool. He who had often escaped great dangers perished miserably."

TOO POSH TO WASH

It is clear that medieval standards of hygiene were not high but given the poor living conditions of the majority of people, the maintenance of personal hygiene was not easy, nor was it considered especially desirable. Fleas, lice, halitosis, and all-round grubbiness were apparently a fact of life for everyone from the monarch downward. It is interesting to see this record from King John's household accounts in 1210, which record several payments to William the Ewerer, the man who gave the king a bath. Between June and November, John traveled between Nottingham and Gloucester, and William was on the royal payroll for 140 days at a daily rate of half a penny. He was paid an additional five-and-a half pence each time the king took a bath and the household accounts record four baths in this period: "To the same William for a bath of the lord king taken at Marlborough, 5½d; for a second bath at Nottingham, 5½d; for a third bath at Northampton, 5½d; for a fourth bath at Gloucester, 5½d." Three hundred years later, Elizabeth I apparently took a bath every three months whether she needed it or not, but her ancestor seems to have been more scrupulous in his bathing habits.

Pomp and ceremony

Edward II was universally reviled for his displays of favoritism. He promoted useless, corrupt, and greedy men into positions of power and emptied the royal coffers by showering Piers Gaveston and others with expensive gifts. Recent wars with Scotland meant that the royal finances were depleted and honest men feared for the state of the realm. Despite his unpopularity, Gaveston was not a man to hide from the limelight. Many of the nobles threatened to boycott Edward's coronation if Gaveston was present, so Edward promised to keep him away. His plans somehow went awry, as Piers was not only there, but played an important part in the ceremonial, carrying the crown and "so decked out that he more resembled the god Mars than an ordinary mortal."

heavy guilt trip

James IV of Scotland (r. 1488–1513) allied himself with the Scottish nobles who wanted to depose his father. He agreed to support their cause as long as James III was not harmed, but he was murdered after the battle of Sauchieburn in 1488. James IV felt so guilty about his involvement in his father's death that he wore a heavy iron chain around his waist as penance. Every year, on the anniversary of the death, James added another weight to the chain.

James was reputedly a cultured man and was interested in science and alchemy. One of his courtiers, the Italian Abbot John Damien claimed to be a proficient alchemist but he is best remembered for his botched attempt to fly. In 1507 he constructed a pair of wings and launched himself from the walls of Stirling Castle intending to fly to France. His fall was broken by a dung heap, which probably saved him from serious injury, although he did break three bones. He blamed his failure on the fact that the he had used the feathers of a hen, a flightless bird, to make the wings.

death duties

Richard III's reputation remains poor, despite the efforts of revisionist historians to prove that he did not murder his nephews the "Princes in the Tower." Perhaps a true glimpse of his character is the account of his behavior on the eve of the battle of Bosworth. "Issuing from his tent by twilight, he observed a centinel [sic] asleep, and is said to have stabbed him, with this remark, 'I found him asleep and have left him as I found him.'" The historian William Hutton goes on to remark, "Perhaps this is the only person Richard ever put to death who deserved it."

ageing gracefully

Elizabeth I was extremely conscious of the image she projected to the world and guarded it jealously. In her portraits she almost seems to become younger and more splendid with the passing years, but by the end of her reign, the reality was a little different. The French ambassador Monsieur de Maisse reported in 1597 that although the Queen was dressed magnificently and adorned with rubies and pearls, her face beneath a "great reddish-coloured wig," "appears to be very aged" [not surprising as Elizabeth was 64 at the time] and "is long and thin and her teeth are very yellow and unequal compared with what they were formerly, so they say, and on the left side less than on the right. Many of them are missing so that one cannot understand her easily when she speaks quickly. Her figure is fair and tall and graceful in whatever she does; so far as may be she keeps her dignity, yet humbly and graciously withal."

death becomes her

For centuries royal marriages were often political affairs, conducted for the purposes of national diplomacy rather than because of emotional attachments on the part of the leading players. In 1599 King Henri IV of France divorced his wife of 20 years and married the 15-year-old Marie de Medici in a calculated move to ally himself with the previous royal dynasty, the Valois. He also needed to provide an heir to the French throne. Unfortunately, his wife was one of the few woman not swayed by the king's legendary charms, and Marie found that the only way she could cope with the king's amorous embraces was to smother herself in perfume. When Henri died after 10 years of marriage, killed by an assassin, Marie struggled to hide her delight as she became Regent for her nine-year-old son Louis XIII.

history bites

wisest fool in christendom

Given James I's parentage, it is perhaps not surprising that he was wary of assassination. The son of Mary Queen of Scots and Henry, Lord Darnley, James was born in 1566; his father was probably murdered on his mother's orders and his mother was beheaded by Elizabeth I. James was brought up by various Scottish nobles in an era of religious intrigue and political instability. However, he survived to successfully rule Scotland as James VI, and from 1603, he ruled England too. Aged 37 when he inherited the English throne from Elizabeth I, he was an object of curiosity to the English, many of whom regarded the Scots as little more than northern barbarians. Descriptions such as this one, which described how he wore padded clothes to protect himself from assassins, did not disappoint: "He was of a middle stature, more corpulent through his clothes then in his body, yet fat enough, his clothes ever being made large and easy, the Doublets quilted for steletto proofe, [to be dagger-proof] his Breeches in great pleats and full stuffed ... His Beard was very thin. His Tongue too large for his mouth, which ever made him speak full in the mouth, and made him drink very uncomely, as if eating his drink, which came out into the cup of each side of his mouth." (The author of this description, Sir Arthur Wilson, was clerk to the kitchen for James I, but was dismissed in 1617 for writing a satire on the Scots.)

Royal Encounters

French Influence

Henrietta Maria (1609–1669), the consort of Charles I, appears to have embodied many French stereotypes: she was elegant, vivacious, opinionated, and believed France was the center of the universe. She was far from popular in England, principally because of her Catholic religion, and contemporaries thought that she exerted some sort of malign Popish influence over the vacillating king. After a shaky start, their marriage was a great success in that the king and queen genuinely came to love each other. Henrietta Maria did not have an easy life given the Civil War and murder of her husband by the Puritans, but she was resolutely cheerful in the face of exile and (comparative) poverty. Whenever she traveled by ship, it seemed that the weather always turned against her, so much so that her children referred to the storms as "*Maman*'s weather." During one particularly rough Channel crossing in 1643, the Queen regarded her sickly retinue with amusement, cheeringly saying "Comfort yourselves, *mes chères*, Queens of England are never drowned."

Royal Salt

Charles I displayed great dignity at the time of his death and after his execution, his corpse was sewn back together so that relatives could view the body prior to burial. He was interred at St. George's Chapel

history bites

Windsor in the same tomb as Henry VIII, although somehow the coffin "disappeared" for many years. In 1813 the royal physician Sir Henry Halford rediscovered it, and could not resist stealing the king's fourth cervical vertebra, which had been cleanly sliced in two. Sir Henry did not hide his treasure away: he used it as a saltcellar for 30 years.

Royal Kiss

Royal remains seem to have exerted a curious fascination over lesser mortals for generations. Samuel Pepys recalled that in 1669 the mummified remains of Henry V's queen, Katherine of Valois were displayed at Westminster Abbey. "...here we did see, by particular favour, the body of Queen Katherine of Valois, and had her upper part of her body in my hands. And I did kiss her mouth, reflecting upon it that I did kiss a Queen, and that this was my birthday, 36 years old, that I did first kiss a Queen."

wine, women, and song

Charles II has become known for his great charm and love of women. After the austerity of the years of Puritan rule, his reign (1660–1685) is often seen as one of unbridled debauchery. It was not without political and religious problems and conflicts between

Royal Encounters

Catholics and Protestants remained ever-present. The king's affections were entirely without religious prejudice, however, although the majority of the population distrusted Catholics and would not countenance a Catholic monarch. At the time of the Popish Plot in 1678, an angry mob surrounded a coach that they believed contained Louise de Kéroualle, the king's French, Catholic mistress. They were surprised when the very English Nell Gwynne stuck her head out in an effort to calm the crowd. "Pray good people be civil," she said. "I am the Protestant whore."

Royal Protection

Charles himself remained a relatively popular monarch, unlike his brother and heir James, Duke of York, who was regarded as a dour, charmless, and overly ambitious man. Charles was accustomed to stroll in Hyde Park, sometimes accompanied by only one or two companions. One morning he met his brother James who pointed out that it was positively dangerous for the king to walk in public places without some sort of protection. Charles disagreed, "There is no danger," he said, "no man in England would do me harm to make you king."

history bites

bleeding loss

As Duke of York, James II had undoubtedly proved he was a brave commander, leading troops into battle against the Dutch in the 1670s. His reign was cut short, however, by his refusal to renounce Catholicism, an act that was intolerable to the mass of English people unused to religious tolerance. In 1688 his son-in-law William of Orange led an invasion force to drive James into exile. One of the reasons William succeeded is that at the critical moment, when James should have been gathering his forces around him, he suffered from a series of incapacitating nosebleeds that confined him to bed.

drunken rage

History is littered with tales of monarchs crazed by illness, defective genes, or simply power. Murad IV (1612–1640) who ruled the Ottoman Empire from 1623 to 1640 seems to have been blighted by all three problems. Although he was undeniably cruel, he worked to re-establish royal authority and is remembered as one of the more successful sultans. On a personal level, however, he was almost psychotic and paranoid to the point of having three of his brothers murdered so that they could not threaten his power. He locked his surviving brother Ibrahim in a cage on the grounds that he was too mad to be considered a threat. He prohibited smoking, and the consumption of coffee or alcohol throughout the empire, on pain of execution, although he often indulged in these habits himself. Somewhat ironically for a ruler who banned alcohol, Murad was a chronic alcoholic, and wine and spirits simply turned him into a maniac. It was reported that he would run "through the streets barefooted with only a loose gown around him, like a madman," and that he "killed whoever came his way." He took particular pleasure in beheading men with fat necks. He roamed the streets accompanied by his executioner, simply killing people on a whim and executed some 25,000 over five years. Fortunately for the population of Turkey, Murad died of cirrhosis of the liver and was succeeded by Ibrahim, the brother he had deemed too mad to threaten him. Ibrahim's reaction to his brother's death was to dance through the harem shouting, "The butcher of the empire is dead!"

mood swings

Another unfortunate heir was Don Carlos of Spain, the son of Philip II and his wife Maria Manuela of Portugal. Carlos suffered from an over-abundance of Habsburg genes: his parents were double first cousins, and because of intense inter-marriage among his forbears, he only had four great-grandparents, rather than the usual eight. Many of his problems may be attributed to in-breeding, and they were exacerbated by his difficult birth. Hunchbacked, with one leg considerably shorter than the other, Carlos demonstrated aggressive mood swings and retarded mental development. He grew up to be sadistic and cruel and the royal accounts show payments of money made to the fathers of girls "beaten by the orders of His Highness." A shoemaker who presented Carlos with a pair of boots was forced to cut them up and eat them just because they displeased the prince.

Heir to the Spanish half of the Habsburg empire, Carlos was obviously not ideal kingly material and his father wrote in a letter to the Pope, "It has been God's will that the prince should have such great and numerous defects, partly mental, partly due to his physical condition, utterly lacking as he is in the qualifications necessary for ruling, I saw the grave risks which would arise were he to be given the succession." Having plotted to kill his father, Carlos was imprisoned in Arévalo castle where he died in 1568, apparently "of his own excesses," although many suspected that Philip had him slowly poisoned.

calming influence

Louis XIV of France demonstrated an extraordinary arrogance throughout his long life (1638–1715), only too aware of the importance of his position in the world. When his father playfully asked him: "What is your name?" the four-year-old Prince Louis firmly replied, "Louis XIV." "Not yet" his father replied, although within a year Louis XIII was dead, leaving the throne to his son, who was, indeed, Louis XIV.

In 1704, enraged by the news of the French defeat at Blenheim at the hands of the British under Marlborough, Louis ranted, "How could God do this to me, after all I have done for him?"

Louis XIV became rather more devout and conservative in old age and this alteration in outlook has been attributed to the influence of his second wife, the redoubtable Madame de Maintenon. Originally employed as a governess to Louis's illegitimate children by an earlier mistress, Madame de Montespan, Francoise d'Aubigné's quiet piety and decency impressed both the king and his queen Marie-Thérèse. Indeed Marie-Thérèse died in the arms of Madame de Maintenon in 1683 and declared that she had never been so well treated by her husband since the arrival of Maintenon. Some time in the winter of 1685–1686 Louis married Madame de Maintenon and they grew old together. When Madame de Maintenon was 75 and the king 70, she complained to her confessor that she found it very tiring when the king wished to make love to her twice a day.

Madame de Maintenon was not ashamed of her roots in the petit-bourgeoisie and must have found the strict court etiquette of Versailles trying at times. When walking around the beautiful gardens at Versailles, a lady-in-waiting remarked that the king's prized carp, housed in an exquisite pond, seemed rather listless. "They are like me," Madame de Maintenon replied, "They miss their native mud."

unruly behaviour

Peter the Great of Russia traveled to Holland in 1697 where he learned about everything from shipbuilding to surgery. He became fascinated by anatomy and studied with the greatest professor of the day, Fredrik Ruysch. The Tsar considered himself a qualified surgeon after his hours with Ruysch and in the years to come, always carried a case of surgical instruments with him. His staff were loath to report any illnesses to him, in case the tsar offered—or insisted—on intervening with his "expertise."

Peter moved on to London and stayed in the house of John Evelyn the noted diarist. Evelyn was proud of his house, and especially the garden, which he had spent 45 years laying out. Sadly, the Russians were uninterested not only in horticulture, but also in Evelyn's taste in interior design. Evelyn's steward was aghast at the destruction they caused: "There is a house full of people and right nasty," he wrote, who managed to break windows, burn all the chairs, and use the pictures for target practice. The gardens looked "as if a regiment of soldiers in iron shoes had drilled on it" and the magnificent hedge had suffered as the tsar delighted in shoving his friends through it in wheelbarrow races. After the Russians had left,

Evelyn was compensated to the tune of £350—an enormous sum for the time.

The excesses of Peter the Great's court were legendary and were certainly daunting for foreigners unused to the Tsar's ways. Before an audience with the monarch, guests were expected to drink a pint of sherry, which was usually handed to them by a trained bear. The Hanoverian Ambassador, Friederich Weber spent seven years in St. Petersburg and published a detailed account of his time in Russia. He reported on the enormous amount of alcohol consumed by courtiers, and after he had finished one lavish meal by sinking a full quart of brandy, he blearily noted: "I had the comfort to observe that the rest of the guests lying asleep on the floor were in no condition to make reflections on my little skill in drinking."

Vertically Challenged

William III was not physically blessed, being short and hump-backed. Married to his cousin Mary, the daughter of James II of England, one wag commented that, "He hung on her arm like a bracelet." However, he was brave in battle, intelligent, and lucky. In 1689 he led the first successful invasion of England since 1066 to capture the English throne, while still retaining his Dutch possessions. The Glorious Revolution and the coronation of William and Mary as joint monarchs meant that William had to spend more time in England, a country he disliked and where he was unpopular. "I am sure this people has not been made for me, not I for it," he complained.

empty prince

Charles II on Prince George, husband of Queen Anne: "I have tried him drunk, and I have tried him sober; and there is nothing in him."

tomcatting around

When Louis XIV died after 72 years on the throne, he was succeeded by his great-grandson, the five-year-old Louis XV. The boy's uncle, Philip Duc d'Orleans acted as Regent during the minority, and he was a man noted above all for his womanizing. His own mother remarked that he was "crazy about women" and that "he troubles little about their looks." When pressed on this last point, the charming Duc replied, "*Bah Maman*, at night all cats are grey."

toy soldiers at bedtime

Catherine the Great's reputation has always been rather mixed. Unsavory stories circulated about her behavior during her lifetime (1729–1796) and have livened up the history books ever since. She was married at the age of 16 to the Grand Duke Peter, heir to the Russian throne, a man who was probably mentally unstable and apparently lacking in the good looks customary for a Prince Charming. At the very least his behavior was that of a boorish lout. After eight years of marriage, Catherine and Peter had failed to produce an heir. Peter's habit of playing with toy soldiers in bed may have had something to do with it. His tutor wrote: "His Imperial Highness must be taught not to make ugly faces at people, not to hold indecorous conversations with his inferiors and not to empty his wine glass over the heads of the footmen who wait at table."

UNFIT TO RULE

As opponents of the hereditary principal are keen to point out, many of the occupants of high office are simply unfit to govern, and the Emperor Ferdinand I of Austria was probably a good example. He once remarked, "It is easy to govern, but what is difficult is to sign one's name." His favorite occupation was to cram himself into a wastepaper basket and roll around the palace like a ball. Ferdinand was certainly epileptic and probably struggled with learning difficulties, but he succeeded to the Imperial throne in 1835 and neatly summarized his regal position: "I am the Emperor. I want noodles, so I get them."

history bites

dysfunctional monarchy

The Hanoverian monarchs were something of a dysfunctional family; the children rarely got on with their parents and for several generations, the heir to the throne and incumbent monarch all seemed to enjoy particularly bitter relations. George II's antagonism toward his father had a great deal to do with the fact that George I imprisoned his wife in Germany for 32 years and prevented his children from contacting her. In his turn, George II despised his own son, Frederick, Prince of Wales, damning him with the words: "Our son is the greatest ass, the greatest liar and the greatest beast in the whole world, and we wish he was out of it." The king's wish was granted. Frederick predeceased his father by nine years, when he was killed by a tennis ball in 1751.

popular words

When Charlotte of Mecklenberg-Strelitz arrived in England in 1761 for her marriage to George III, the members of the court studied her intently. Horace Walpole gave her a broadly favorable write-up, noting that she was "not tall, nor a beauty; pale and very thin; but looks sensible; and is genteel." Although she was German, the language was not a barrier as the house of Hanover then occupied the English throne and their Teutonic origins were often the butt of jokes among the satirists of the day. As Charlotte began to chat with her new family, they discussed the various German dialects and the King said he believed that Hanoverian was a very pure one. "Oh no Sir," said the Queen, "it is the worst of all." Walpole wryly noted, "She will not be unpopular."

GREAT SCRIBBLER

The historian Edward Gibbon (1737–1794) published the first volume of his monumental *Decline and Fall of the Roman Empire* in 1776 and presented a copy to the king's brother, the Duke of Gloucester. He finished the second volume in 1781 and the Duke received it cheerily, saying, "Another damned thick square book! Always scribble, scribble, scribble! Eh! Mr Gibbon!"

FAT CHANCE

When George Prince of Wales (the future George IV) was finally compelled to marry and produce an heir, his bride was his cousin, Princess Caroline of Brunswick. George was a man of great refinement and good taste, whereas his bride struggled to maintain a minimum level of personal hygiene. The diplomat Lord Malmesbury who orchestrated the marriage noted "she wore coarse petticoats, coarse shifts and thread stockings, and these were never well washed, or changed often enough." Malmesbury worked hard to get Caroline scrubbed up to royal standards, but after the Prince of Wales met her for the first time, he retreated to another room calling out to his servant, "Harris, I am not well; pray get me a glass of brandy." Caroline was famously outspoken and she retorted in French that she thought the prince very fat and not nearly as handsome as his portrait.

jealous dog

Napoleon and Josephine were famous for the grand passion of their early love. On their wedding night, however, Napoleon was attacked by Josephine's dog, Fortuné who thought that the consul was attacking his mistress and bit him on the calf. Napoleon suffered permanent scarring as a result.

disloyal royal

"A Republican by principle and devotion," said Jean-Baptiste Bernadotte in his youth, "I will, until my death, oppose all Royalists and all enemies of my Government and the Republic." Bernadotte (1763–1844) was one of Napoleon's marshals and enjoyed an interesting, if controversial, career. He was eventually sacked by Napoleon, and in a staggering display of treachery, went to fight for the enemy, Charles XIII of Sweden. When the king died in 1818, Bernadotte, who had the phrase "*Mort aux Rois*" (Death to Kings) tattooed on his arm, became King Charles XIV of Sweden and founded the dynasty that still rules the country.

strength of a giant

Tsar Alexander III of Russia was a giant of a man standing at least 6 ft, 6 in. tall. He possessed a strength to match his height and was apparently able to bend silver coins in half. More usefully, after he and his family were involved in a train crash, Alexander was able to hold up the roof of their wrecked carriage, enabling his family to escape to safety. When an Austrian ambassador tried to put diplomatic pressure on Russia and remarked that the Austrian may be forced to mobilize troops near the Russian border, Alexander picked up his fork, twisted a knot in it, tossed it at the ambassador, and said, "That is what I will do with your divisions."

hidden beauty

The Emperor Franz Joseph II of Austria fell in love with his 15-year-old cousin Elisabeth the moment he met her and adored her to the day she died. Known as Sisi, Elizabeth was a great beauty and, as she grew older, worked hard to retain her good looks. She was a proficient equestrian and loved exercise. What she hated was court protocol and she traveled widely around Europe incognito to escape the Habsburg court at Vienna. She disliked being stared at and at the age of 32, declared that she would sit for no more portraits and avoided being photographed. Franz Joseph wrote to her incessantly, constantly worried about her health and the dangers of assassins. After the tragic death of their son Crown Prince Rudolf and later her cousin Ludwig II of Bavaria, she was heard to mutter "May death take me unawares," a wish that was sadly fulfilled.

In 1898 Luigi Luccheni, an Italian anarchist, was stalking the Duke of Orleans, hoping to assassinate him in the name of "freedom." Stranded at Lake Geneva and disappointed by the departure of his ducal victim, Luccheni cast around for another prominent figure to publicize his cause. Sisi was in the wrong place at the wrong time, and indeed, was the wrong victim. On September 10, Luccheni stabbed the Empress while she was walking along the quayside, although at first Sisi was barely aware that anything was amiss. It was only when she suddenly collapsed several minutes later and her corsets were loosened, that her lady-in-waiting realized what had happened, but by then, it was too late. The Empress Elisabeth was dead.

Royal Encounters

we are amused

Queen Victoria's reputation as a woman without a sense of humor stems from all the photographs and portraits in which she appears dignified and unsmiling, yet it is clear from her writings that she had a very finely developed sense of the ridiculous. During one dinner, the Queen sat next to a rather deaf and very dull admiral who regaled the Queen with naval stories, with especial reference to the condition of an old ship which had broken down and been towed into Portsmouth harbor. In an attempt to change the subject, the Queen enquired, "How is your dear sister?"—a question that the admiral obviously didn't hear, because he continued in the same naval vein, saying "She'll be alright when we've turned her over and scraped the barnacles off her bottom." The Queen's shoulders shook helplessly with laughter as she buried her face in her napkin.

throwing caution to the wind

Life as a very minor royal should be reasonably easy—one should be able to live in comfort buttressed against the troubles that afflict lesser mortal by titles, estates, and money. However, boredom occasionally sets in, which often leads to bad behavior and more than one royal schoolboy has proved to be a bit of a handful. Prince Francis of Teck, the younger brother of Queen Mary, began his career as the family black sheep when he was expelled from Wellington College for throwing the headmaster over a hedge. He was charitably described as having a great zest for life, which meant that he became rather too fond of gambling in adulthood. After he lost £10,000 on one race, he was sent to live quietly and cheaply in India, where his cousin Queen Victoria hoped he "would be very steady in every way and resist temptation." Suffice to say that he didn't. His final act of defiance was to bestow the family jewels on his mistress.

Waiter, Waiter

Edward VII was a stickler for the fine nuances of royal protocol and although he was very indulgent toward his grandchildren, he insisted on perfect manners at all times. When his four-year-old grandson, the future Edward VIII, interrupted him during lunch, the child was asked to wait until his grandfather had finished speaking. The poor child could barely contain himself, and shouted "Grandpa, Grandpa!" again. The King patiently asked him to wait his turn and a short while later turned to his grandson and asked what he had wanted. "I was going to tell you there was a caterpillar on your lettuce, but it's all right—you've eaten it," said the young prince.

Royal Encounters

Wrong Turning

The assassination of the heir to the Habsburg Empire in 1914 was the catalyst that began World War I. During his visit to Sarajevo on June 28, Archduke Franz Ferdinand survived one attack as a Serb threw a bomb at his car that bounded off harmlessly. However, fate was against the archduke. The only reason that the eventual assassin got a clear shot at his victim was because the royal driver took a wrong turning and was forced to reverse down a narrow street. Had the driver stuck to the agreed route, the Serb nationalist Gavrilo Princip is unlikely to have been close enough to the royal party to kill him.

George and the Dragon

George V was one of Great Britain's more dignified monarchs and one of the few who led an entirely blameless private life. Indeed, when H. G. Wells criticized his "alien and uninspiring court" during World War I, the king thundered that: "I may be uninspiring, but I'll be damned if I'm an alien!" In middle age, he was a man of great integrity, but as a boy he had been sent away to join the navy. Like many other upper-class contemporaries, he had acquired an impressive set of tattoos—the first was an elaborate dragon on his left arm.

history bites

plowing on

During World War II, Queen Mary was evacuated to the Gloucestershire countryside, where she stayed with her niece, the Duchess of Beaufort, on the Badminton estate. Although a reluctant evacuee and a lifelong "townie," Queen Mary soon adjusted to her circumstances and began to do all she could to support the war effort. Scrap metal was collected all over Britain and recycled for use in munitions manufacture and Queen Mary enthusiastically toured the countryside looking for scrap iron. One day, however, it became clear that the royal fervor had been rather too strong. A servant presented a note to the Queen, which read, "Please Your Majesty, a Mr. Hodge has arrived and he says Your Majesty has taken his plough, and will Your Majesty graciously give it back to him, please, at once, as he can't get on without it."

slight understatement

Emperor Hirohito of Japan (1901–1989) was the 124th emperor in direct succession to the Chrysanthemum Throne. Revered as a god, he assumed the name Showa when he acceded in 1926. It is ironic, given the events of the mid-20th century, that this translates as "enlightened peace." He was a groundbreaking emperor in many ways, however, being the first to travel abroad (his ancestors had stayed in Japan for the preceding 2,700 years) and earning a reputation as a marine biologist. The most testing period of his reign must surely have been at the end of the World War II when the military hierarchy was forced to surrender after America had attacked Japan with the atom bomb. On this occasion, Hirohito made his first radio broadcast and, for the first time, his subjects heard the voice of their emperor. He spoke cautiously in the formal language of the Imperial Court and used magnificent understatement to break the bad news: "The war situation has developed not necessarily to Japan's advantage."

Queen Mother

Queen Elizabeth, the Queen Mother (1900–2002), was famous for her genial manner and wide-ranging cultural tastes. According to her grandson Prince Charles, she was especially fond of Edwardian music hall songs and would sing them to her young grandchildren as she tucked them up in bed. One of her favorites was *Cock of the North*, with its irreverent lyrics, "Auntie Mary had a canary, /Up the leg o' her drawers."

acts of faith

making hell

Many of the early Church Fathers, the scholars who pondered and established liturgy and doctrine in the first 500 years of Christianity's existence, lived colorful lives as young men and adopted the quieter ways of Christianity as they matured. Born to a pagan father, St. Augustine (354–430) grew up in North Africa in a colonial outpost of the Roman Empire in what is now Algeria.

His mother was a Christian, and it was she who gave him his faith. He was well educated and, while studying in Carthage as a young man, acquired a mistress by whom he had a son. It is probably his happy memories of his youth that prompted the most famous lines in St. Augustine's Prayer, "Give me chastity and continence. But not yet."

Augustine moved to Rome in 384 to devote himself to full-time scholarship and was once asked: "What was God doing through all the eternity of time before He created heaven and earth?" "Creating hell," he replied, "for those who ask questions like you."

mass rebuke

St. Ambrose (*c.* 339–397) was a contemporary of St. Augustine (he actually baptized him) and a Roman nobleman who belonged to the ruling elite; his family was Christian, but he was not baptized as a child. In about 371, he became governor of the provinces of Aemilia and Liguria, with his headquarters at Mediolanum, present-day Milan. In the winter of 373, Ambrose was called to the cathedral to settle a dispute between rival factions of Christians and Arians who were both bent on having their candidate installed as bishop. Ambrose succeeded in avoiding a riot by calming the mob, but was then surprised to hear himself nominated for the episcopal post. Although he pointed out that he had never been baptized, let alone ordained as a priest, and could not, therefore, accept, it seemed to be the only way to solve the problem. Ambrose was baptized, ordained, and enthroned within the space of eight days and remained bishop until his death almost quarter of a century later.

Milan's position at the center of the western empire gave Ambrose great influence and he even dared to rebuke the Emperor Theodosius when he tried to enter the cathedral sanctuary during mass. "The Emperor is in the church," Ambrose told Theodosius, "not over it."

history bites

holy roast

The early Christian martyr St. Lawrence was born in Spain and became a deacon in Rome during the third century AD. He refused to surrender the church's treasures to the Emperor Valerian and was condemned to death in 258 by being slowly roasted on a bed of hot coals. He somehow remained reasonably cheerful throughout the whole torment and was asked if he had any last requests. His final words were "Turn me, I am roasted on one side." His stoicism and composure so impressed those who were watching that several Roman senators embraced Christianity on the spot and were followed by hundreds more citizens the next day, which was probably not the result the authorities had intended.

Ritual Pain

St. Patrick (c. 389–461) conducted the baptism of the Irish king Aengus, but during the ceremony he accidentally leaned on his staff and stabbed the king badly in the foot. After the ceremony, St. Patrick realized that king was bleeding rather badly and apologized, asking why the king had not cried out or complained. "I thought it was part of the ritual," Aengus replied.

ACTS OF FAITH

EGG RESTORATION

Swithin, Bishop of Winchester to the Anglos-Saxons, died in 862 and, before his death, modestly asked that his remains be buried outside Winchester Cathedral, rather than inside, "in a place made vile both by the feet of passers-by and by the raindrops falling from the eaves." His wishes were carried out, despite the great esteem in which he was held, but in 971, when the cathedral was rebuilt, the monks tried to move his bones to a more exalted place. The day chosen for the exhumation was July 15, but the plans had to be abandoned because of torrential rains. Forty days later, when the rain had barely ceased, the monks got the hint and decided to leave Swithin where he lay. It is still traditional to believe that if it rains on July 15 (St. Swithin's day), the bad weather will continue for a further 40 days.

The usual miracles are attributed to St. Swithin, such as curing the sick and lame, but almost more impressive is the story that he restored a basket of shattered eggs belonging to a poor woman with no other source of income.

UNLUCKY KING WENCESLAS

The patron saint of the Czech Republic is the medieval king Wenceslas, the same man remembered in the popular Christmas carol. Born in Bohemia in 907, Wenceslas inherited the throne while still a child, and his mother acted as Regent. Wenceslas was raised as a Christian by his grandmother St. Ludmilla, but when his pagan mother was in power she outlawed Christian practices (and killed her mother-in-law for good measure in 921). When Wenceslas took over in 924, he allowed German missionaries to preach in Bohemia and reintroduced Christian worship, which is why he is known as "Good" King Wenceslas. Unfortunately, he was also unlucky, as he was murdered by his pagan brother just five years later while on the way to mass on St. Stephen's day.

Marital Relations

During the ninth century, the Church tried to impose strict rules on marital relations between husband and wife. Sexual intercourse was prohibited for 40 days before Christmas, 40 days before and eight days after Easter, for eight days after Pentecost, on the eve of important religious festivals, and, naturally, on Sundays, Wednesdays, and Fridays. It was out of the question during pregnancy, for 30 days after the birth of a son, or for 40 days after the birth of a daughter, during a woman's menstrual period, and for five days before taking communion. There were few days left. Many husbands thoughtfully consorted with mistresses to avoid placing their wives in a state of sin.

acts of Faith

hellish forks

The fork was first introduced as an eating implement in about 1000 AD. Like many new inventions, it was regarded with suspicion and was actually banned by the Church on the grounds that God had given people fingers to eat with and they should not spurn them in favor of a mere manmade implement. Forks arrived in Europe when the Venetian Doge, Domenico Selvo, married a Byzantine princess in the 11th century. Her habit of eating with a fork was regarded as scandalous and heretical, and her untimely death shortly after her arrival was regarded as divine punishment.

dangerous liaisons

The Knights Templar were a monastic order of knights formed in 1099 at the end of the First Crusade with the purpose of protecting pilgrims en route to the Holy Land. The great reformist monk St. Bernard of Clairvaux (1090–1153) helped to establish the order and wrote the first rules, which were based on those of the Cistercian monks (whose order he founded). Knights were expected to live as monks, simply, modestly, and without recourse to idle gossip or carousing. Celibacy was, of course, the norm and monks were forbidden "to look too much upon the face of woman." Indeed, the knightly rule labored the point and regarded the lure of women as almost as dangerous as fighting the infidel. The bravery of the Templars on the field of battle was legendary, but it was far harder to face: "The company of women [which] is a dangerous thing, for by it the old devil has led many from the straight path of paradise . . . For this reason none of you may presume to kiss a woman, be it widow, young girl, mother, sister, aunt, or any other; and henceforth the Knighthood of Jesus Christ should avoid at all costs the embrace of women, by which men have perished many times."

Larger than Life

The eminent medieval religious philosopher St. Thomas Aquinas (1225–1274) was born into a noble family, a younger son of Count Landulf of Aquino, near Naples. He was educated at the monastery of Monte Cassino and at the university of Naples, but in 1244, he shocked his aristocratic family with his decision to join the new mendicant order of monks, the Dominicans. His brothers were so appalled by his adoption of a low life that they kidnapped Thomas and imprisoned him in the family castle for a year. Thomas refused to change his plans and his brothers' attempts to introduce a love interest didn't help: he chased his seducer from the room with a poker. He finally escaped to the university of Paris where he became something of an institution—literally and metaphorically. He grew so fat that the dining-room table had a semi-circle cut out of it to accommodate his enormous girth.

good from evil

During the Albigensian Crusade (1209–1229), in an attempt to root out proponents of the Cathar heresy in southern France, a French army under Simon de Montfort besieged Béziers. When the siege collapsed and the French were on the verge of sacking the town, the soldiers wanted to know how to distinguish between heretics and good Christians. De Montfort hesitated, then said "Kill them all, the Lord will know his own."

shooting stars

The appearance of shooting stars or comets in medieval times was rarely a cause for rejoicing. They were associated with many superstitions, almost all of them heralding misfortune and disaster. In 975, the *Anglo-Saxon Chronicle* bleakly recorded the appearance of a comet which "spread God's vengeance throughout the land, and famine scoured the hills" and in 1066, the appearance of Halley's comet heralded the English defeat at the Battle of Hastings. It was not until 1577 that the Danish astronomer Tycho Brahe dispelled more practical fears by proving that comets were phenomena of space rather than the earth's atmosphere. So when a comet appeared in 1456, Pope Calixtus III was merely protecting the faithful by publishing a Papal Bull asking Christendom to pray that the comet, which he called "a symbol of the anger of God" be diverted—preferably against the Turks, who were threatening the boundaries of western Europe.

Pay For your Soul

The Renaissance scholar and theologian Desiderius Erasmus (1466–1536) was noted for his criticism of the corruption within the medieval Catholic Church and his works influenced the advance of the Protestant Reformation. In his teachings, Erasmus was reacting to remarks such as this from the cynical Pope Julius II, "God will forgive you anything—if you pay me enough money." Erasmus believed that Christian faith should be based on the teachings of the Scriptures rather than the diktats of the clergy, so when a colleague reproached him for not observing the Lenten fast, Erasmus replied, "I have a Catholic soul, but a Lutheran stomach."

Losing Face

Lawyer, writer, humanist scholar, and politician, Sir Thomas More (1477–1535) became Henry VIII's Lord Chancellor—the highest post in the land, in 1529. He amassed a reasonable fortune, but was also a man of sincere and devout religious beliefs and when called upon to renounce the Pope's authority in England, he resigned his public offices and tried to live quietly in Chelsea from 1532. He was imprisoned in the Tower of London by the king in 1535, accused of high treason. His wife, who was a far more down-to-earth person could not understand what she regarded as his stubbornness in refusing to acknowledge the king's supremacy over the Church: "I marvel that you, that have been always hitherto taken for so wise a man, will now play the fool to lie in this close filthy prison...when you might be abroad at your liberty," she said when visiting him in prison. More was not swayed by her imprecations and was beheaded later in the year.

driving offense

The Holy Days and Fasting Act of 1551 made it compulsory for everyone to attend church on the annual "nativitie of our Lorde," but they had to walk to get there. Any vehicle used for church going on Christmas Day was to be confiscated and sold, with the money going toward poor relief. This law remains unrepealed in Britain so, in theory, anyone who drives a car to church on Christmas Day is committing an offense.

history bites

saintly relics

Philip II of Spain (1527–1598) was renowned for the intensity of his Catholic faith, which governed his life and work. It is said that he possessed more than 7,000 holy relics, which included 144 heads, 306 arms, and ten whole bodies. As he lay dying, he called for the arm of St. Vincent and the knee of St. Sebastian to sustain him.

beard tax

In the Russian Orthodox religion, beards were regarded as a sign of religious belief and male self-respect. In the mid-17th century, the tsars tried to relax the rules and men were permitted to shave if they so wished. The Patriarch Adrian condemned this decision, however, saying: "God did not create men beardless, only cats and dogs. Shaving is not only foolishness and dishonor; it is mortal sin." Peter the Great had different views and as part of his efforts to modernize Russia he went further: if a man arrived at court with a beard, he inevitably went home without one, roughly shaved by one of the court officials. Eventually, Peter decided that it was easier to impose a tax on those who wished to wear beards; peasants paid two kopeks, while wealthier individuals paid as much as 100 roubles, and those who had paid were entitled to wear a small medallion inscribed with the words "Tax paid."

acts of faith

suspicious minds

Over the centuries, many scientists or proponents of new ideas have suffered at the hands of a suspicious church. Galileo's insistence on the Copernican heresy that the planets move around the sun earned him interrogation by the Inquisition and house arrest. He was made to renounce the Copernican doctrine, but as he rose from his knees, he apparently muttered, "But still it moves," and later remarked that "I do not feel obliged to believe that the same God who has endowed us with sense, reason, and intellect, has intended us to forgo their use." His words were echoed 300 years later by Charles Darwin, who wrote, "I cannot persuade myself that a beneficent and omnipotent God would have designedly created parasitic wasps with the express intention of their feeding within the living bodies of Caterpillars."

prostituting his art

When the great French playwright Molière died suddenly in 1673, the royal court was thrown into confusion. In 17th-century France, acting and theatricals were regarded as trades little better than prostitution, and when an actor was near death, it was customary for him to renounce his profession so that he could be buried in consecrated ground. Molière had died so suddenly that he had not managed this and despite the playwright's exalted reputation, the Archbishop of

Paris would not be swayed on the subject. Madame Molière therefore approached the king, Louis XIV, who solved the problem with his usual pragmatism. He enquired of the church authorities what they considered to be the depth of sacred ground. When he heard that it was 14 feet, the king decreed that Molière's grave should be dug 16 feet deep, "Then it cannot be said that he is buried in consecrated ground, nor need it scandalize the clergy."

hot house

John Wesley (1703–1791), the evangelist and founder of Methodism, preached some 40,000 sermons during his 50-year ministry and traveled an estimated 250,000 miles. Tens of thousands of people gathered to hear him preach as he had a reputation as a powerful orator. During one sermon, however, he was dismayed to see that a few members of the congregation had fallen asleep, so to wake them up, Wesley shouted "Fire! Fire!" "Where?" they called back. "In hell," Wesley replied sternly, "for those who sleep under the preaching of the word."

would you adam and eve it?

Contemporaries regarded the writer and artist William Blake (1757–1827) as something of an eccentric visionary, whose highly original and mystical works contain some of the most beautiful lyricism in the English language. Blake had a real faith in the unseen and believed he was guided by visitations from the spiritual world. In the 1790s, he lived in Lambeth with his wife and was once visited by a friend, who arrived to find Mr. and Mrs. Blake enjoying the sun in the garden while reading Milton's *Paradise Lost*. To add to the realism of the occasion, they were entirely naked. When Blake spotted his friend, he shouted, "Come in! It's only Adam and Eve, you know!"

the good book

The Boston preacher John Cotton (1584–1652), known as the "Patriarch of New England," fled from England to escape persecution for his Puritan faith. He was America's first Congregationalist minister and was responsible for publishing the first children's book in the American colonies in 1646. Predictably it had a religious theme, albeit with a syrupy title: *Spiritual Milk for Boston Babes in either England drawn from the Breasts of Both Testaments for their Souls' Nourishment.*

sin and be forgiven

The American preacher and Congregationalist minister Henry Ward Beecher (1813–1887) advocated temperance and was earnestly opposed to slavery. His faith was not based on strict Calvinist denial, but on a belief in a truly forgiving God. To be truly religious, he told his flock, you must sin occasionally, as Christ cannot save you unless you do.

way out

At the end of his life (1880–1946), the irascible actor and lifelong agnostic W.C. Fields became concerned that there may, after all be an afterlife. He was discovered leafing through a Bible but quickly explained away his unaccustomed religious interest: "I'm looking for a loophole," he said.

bright spark

The scientist Michael Faraday (1791–1867) was a modest and devout man, despite his towering scientific achievements. He belonged to the Sandemanian Church, a fundamentalist sect that believed in a rigid and literal interpretation of the Bible. In 1844, Faraday was expelled from the church because he had failed to attend Sunday service. Faraday had not made the decision lightly—he had been invited to lunch with Queen Victoria and had only reluctantly decided that he should obey his Queen rather than the Church.

acts of faith

meet the Relatives

The impact of Charles Darwin's theory of evolution created a frenzied debate in scientific and religious circles in the mid-19th century. Many people simply could not accept that man was descended from apes, and when asked to comment on the dispute, the politician Benjamin Disraeli announced, "I am on the side of the angels."

Philip Gosse (1810–1888), a highly respected naturalist and deeply religious man, formulated a new theory in an effort to reconcile his religious beliefs with perceived scientific fact. He announced that God had created a universe that *appeared* to have a long history, far longer than the accepted 6,000 years of Biblical history. Thus God had created mountain ranges, put fossils in the rocks, and age rings in trees to create a functioning universe. This was known as the *Omphalos* theory (Greek for navel), which had its roots in the oft-asked question of whether Adam and Eve had navels. Gosse unequivocally declared that they did. Instead of pacifying believers, the *Omphalos* was criticized because it implied fraudulent behavior on the part of the Creator, and Gosse retreated from the fray, depressed and disheartened.

history bites

there in spirit

After Prince Albert died in 1861, his bereft widow Queen Victoria preserved his possessions as though he were still alive, and led her family in commemorating the anniversary of his death on December 14 every year. Her surviving children paid their mother the same courtesy after her death in 1901, and visited her mausoleum at Frogmore near Windsor Castle every year. On one occasion as they knelt in prayer and contemplation, a beautiful white dove flew in. "It is dear Mama's spirit," murmured one princess. "No it is not", replied Princess Louise adamantly, who had noticed something her sisters had not seen. Her sisters persisted, but Louise was certain it could not be: "Dear Mama's spirit would never have ruined Beatrice's hat."

the first Jew

When Denmark was occupied by the forces of Nazi Germany during World War II, Hitler decreed that all Danish Jews should be distinguished by wearing a yellow Star of David armband. Within hours of the publication of the order, almost the entire population of Denmark, of all religious faiths, sported a yellow armband, including the king, Christian X, who proudly declared "I am my country's first Jew."

acts of faith

devout mp

Hilaire Belloc was a gifted writer and a devout Catholic. Born during a thunderstorm two days before the German invasion of France in 1870, his French father died when he was two and he was raised in Britain by his English mother. A critic, novelist, and poet, he is perhaps best remembered for his comic verse, but he was also an MP, standing for Salford in 1906. He knew that his religion may alienate potential voters, so in his first speech, he confronted the problem head-on. "I am a Catholic. As far as possible I go to Mass every day. As far as possible I kneel down and tell these beads every day... If you reject me on account of my religion, I shall thank God that he has spared me the indignity of being your representative." He was elected with a respectable majority.

hitler's dream

As a corporal in World War I, Adolf Hitler dreamed that he was buried inside a huge mound of earth, and awoke with the sensation of dirt in his mouth. He immediately got up and walked outside the dugout, which was flattened by an artillery shell seconds later. Had he stayed in bed, the course of 20th-century history may have been very different. Years later, Hitler delighted in recounting this story to explain how God had saved him for the purpose of leading Germany in the 1930s and 1940s.

eating words

The 19th-century ruler of Ethiopia, Emperor Menelik II, worked hard to modernize his country, introducing modern systems of education, transport, and communications. However, his personal method of health care was eccentric and of dubious value. When he felt ill, he put his faith in the healing power of the Bible and ate a page or two. It does not seem to have harmed him, until in 1913, when he was recovering from a stroke, he ordered his doctors to feed him the entire Old Testament Book of Kings. He was really too ill to eat, and died somewhere around the visit of the Queen of Sheba to Solomon.

the cost of poverty

The Indian spiritual leader Mahatma Gandhi (1869–1948) campaigned for Indian independence by advocating non-violent methods of resistance to British rule. He worked to improve the lives of India's poorest citizens, the "Untouchables" and cooperated with the British over the drafting of a constitution for the independent nation. Gandhi lived an ascetic lifestyle, wearing only a loincloth, eating simply, and traveling on foot or by the cheapest method where possible. Lord Mountbatten, the last viceroy of India, held Gandhi in high regard, but he was aware of the dangers the Mahatma's lifestyle posed: he was vulnerable to attack from extremists because he wished to be constantly visible. When Mountbatten learned that all Gandhi's "Untouchable" companions on one railway trip had been selected and vetted by the security services, he said, "You have no idea what it costs to keep that old man in poverty."

When Gandhi stayed with a friend, she knew he would need supplies of goat's milk, fresh fruit, and other unusual items to sustain him. Like Mountbatten she was surprised at the cost of his Spartan lifestyle: "You've no idea, Mahatma, how expensive it is to provide you with the wherewithal to fast."

catholic humanity

The writer Evelyn Waugh was noted for his prickly temperament, and even those closest to him suffered from his caustic tongue. Nancy Mitford was a life-long friend and after an incident when Waugh was especially spiteful to a young French intellectual at one of her dinner parties, she asked Waugh how he could reconcile his brutal behavior with his Catholic faith. "You have no idea how much nastier I would be if I were not a Catholic," said Waugh. "Without supernatural aid I would hardly be a human being."

xmas vs christmas

Educationalists often deplore the use of abbreviated or slang words, and one of the most commonly used is Xmas, in place of Christmas. Wicked atheists have been blamed for using an X in the place of the word Christ, and thus "taking the Christ out of Christmas." In fact, the reverse is true. The X has been used by theologians for hundreds of years to denote the Greek letter *chi,* the first letter in the Greek spelling of the word Christ. The X represents Christ and the cross upon which he was crucified.

the Presidency

Polite Society

George Washington (1732–1799) had a distinguished career as a soldier (at first in the British army) and had remarkable powers as a leader of men, impressing contemporaries with his essential decency and simplicity of behavior. The writer Nathanial Hawthorne later summed up the popular view when he wrote of Washington, "I imagine he was born with his clothes on and his hair powdered and made a stately bow on his first appearance in the world."

During the Revolutionary War, Washington published *The Rules of Civility and Decent Behavior on Company and Conversation,* a list of sensible advice on basic good manners in the late 18th century. "Kill no vermin or fleas, lice, ticks, etc in the sight of others; if you see any filth or thick spittle put your foot dexterously upon it; if it be upon the clothes of your companions, put it off privately, and if it be upon your own clothes, return thanks to him who puts it off . . . Cleanse not your teeth with the tablecloth, napkin, fork, or knife; but if others do it, let it be done without a peep to them."

history bites

Washington is famous for his lack of teeth—by the time he was inaugurated president he only had one of his own teeth remaining. He never actually owned pair of wooden false teeth, although he used a selection of dentures over the years that were made from the teeth of cows, humans, or hippopotami, or else were fashioned from ivory or lead. Despite, or maybe because of his own lack of teeth, Washington ordered that each of his horses had their teeth cleaned every morning.

all men are tyrants

The influence of first ladies on their husbands is often the source of gossip, debate, and conjecture. Abigail Adams was clearly made of stern stuff and many of her letters to John Adams (the second president, 1796–1800) survive. An intelligent woman, she was only too aware of the importance of the work begun by the Continental Congress in framing the laws of the new United States and submitted this plea to her husband in March 1776. "In the new code of laws which I suppose it will be necessary for you to make I desire you would remember the ladies and be more generous and favorable to them than your ancestors. Do not put such unlimited power into the hands of the husbands. Remember all men would be tyrants if they could."

the Presidency

Fine Wines

Thomas Jefferson (1743–1826) was America's third president from 1801 until 1809 and the author of the Declaration of Independence. A man of remarkably wide interests and talents, he had a penchant for collecting fine wine, or actually, almost any wine. Having retired from public life in 1794, he was persuaded out of retirement in 1797 to act as vice-president. Possibly to help with the vicissitudes of life as president, from 1801 he purchased some 20,000 bottles of wine from Europe.

Jefferson was a man of wide-ranging interests and an enquiring mind. His political achievements are legendary, but he was also a part-time inventor. After his time as US Ambassador to Europe, he returned to America in the 1790s with a love of European cooking, and brought with him recipes for exotic delicacies such as ice cream, macaroni, and macaroons. Among his papers is a diagram of a pasta-making machine, as well as designs for a more efficient plow, a swivel chair, a pedometer, and a letter copying machine.

When Thomas Jefferson was president, diplomacy was often conducted at a stately pace as the distances involved meant that despatches between ambassadors and their political masters traveled very slowly. Jefferson remarked that he had not heard from America's ambassador to Spain for over two years, but was not unduly worried by the man's silence: "If I don't hear from him next year, I will write him a letter," he said.

Rather aptly for the author of the Declaration of Independence, Jefferson died on Independence Day, 1826.

naked truth

John Quincy Adams (president from 1825–1829) habitually swam naked in the Potomac every day at 5 am. Although professional journalists were not as inquisitive as today, Annie Royall, one of the first female journalists, repeatedly tried to gain an interview with Adams. She finally got her way by arriving at the river and sitting on the president's clothes, effectively trapping him in the water, and refusing to leave until he agreed to an interview.

ducking and diving

Annie Royall herself was something of a character. Born in 1769, she wrote a number of pamphlets and books advocating the separation of Church and state. Her gravestone in the Congressional cemetery reads "Annie Royall 1769–1854. Hated Presbytarians; liked all other denominations, and was especially a good friend of the Masons. She was sentenced to be ducked in the Potomac River for her rantings in court."

the Presidency

en-suite quincy

During the early years of the 19th century, standards of hygiene began to improve throughout the western world, as piped water and effective sewers became more common. The White House was obviously an early adopter of such improvements and the first president to enjoy the use of an indoor flushing lavatory was John Quincy Adams. He also enjoyed the dubious privilege of hearing the lavatory or water closet called a "quincy" for a few years, named in his honor.

salt of the earth

Statesman, soldier, and president, Andrew Jackson (1767–1845) did not learn to read until he was 17 and traded on his "salt of the earth" roots. During his victory celebration in 1828, "Old Hickory's" supporters partied at the White House, breaking crockery and trampling on the furniture in their muddy boots, to the dismay of the staff.

the ok president

The eighth president, Martin van Buren (1782–1862) was the first US president who was actually born in the USA. Of Dutch descent, Van Buren came from Kinderhook, New York, a place he often referred to in speeches as "Old Kinderhook." His supporters formed "OK clubs" during his campaign, and OK entered the language to mean "all right."

Martin Van Buren was unpopular in the southern states, especially Virginia where he won only nine votes. His supporters accused the opposition of fraud, to which one wag responded, "Yes, we are still looking for the person who voted nine times!"

haggard harrison

Although President William Henry Harrison (1773–1841) made one of the longest of all inaugural addresses, his term of office in 1841 was the shortest, at only one month. Interestingly, in his address he said he would not be a candidate for a second term. He was the first president to die in office, expiring from pneumonia and exhaustion after a relentless election campaign.

Party pooper

James K. Polk's (1795–1849) family were Irish Protestants from Ulster and he appears to have inherited their puritan inclinations, along with a traditional Protestant work ethic. He disapproved of dancing, disliked any music that wasn't a hymn, and believed that enjoyment and fun were simply a waste of time. He cut short soirées in the

The Presidency

White House by ensuring that no refreshments were served, and his wife banned dancing. Polk was one of the few politicians to fulfill all his campaign pledges, but he ruined his health with overwork, and died of exhaustion just three months after leaving office.

Polk's dislike of frivolity was echoed by one of his successors, Rutherford B. Hayes (1822–1893), who banished wine and liquor from the White House when he assumed office in 1877. Hayes and his wife Lucy were members of the temperance movement and wanted to set a good example to the rest of the country. His wife was nicknamed "Lemonade Lucy," although Hayes insisted that the ban on alcohol was his idea. His schemes were not universally popular and after one state dinner, the Secretary of State William Evarts was heard to remark, "It was a brilliant affair; the water flowed like champagne."

Rough and Ready

Zachary Taylor (1784–1850), the hero of the 1846–1848 Mexican War, a man nicknamed "Old Rough and Ready," and who never lost a battle, was swept to power as president in 1848 in the first election to be held simultaneously in every state. Taylor himself had never even voted in an election; he had never remained in one place long enough to register as a voter and cast his first vote (presumably for himself) aged 62.

history bites

POOR PRESIDENT

Franklin Pierce (1804–1869), the 14th president was a good-looking Democrat from New Hampshire, and was something of a compromise candidate: he was only nominated after the Democratic convention had held a tiring 49 ballots. His presidency was not a distinguished one and was hampered by the president's grief over the death of his only son and his heavy drinking. Shortly before he left office, his long-suffering secretary said, "Whoever may be elected, we cannot get a poorer cuss than now disgraces the presidential chair!"

UNFASHIONABLE TRENDSETTERS

Ulysses S. Grant (1822–1885) was one of the finest Civil War generals, but was a slightly hesitant presidential candidate. His cross-eyed wife Julia was keen to be first lady and when he had taken the Oath of Office, he turned to his wife and said, "Now my dear, I hope you're happy." Julia's earliest act as first lady was to issue a press release saying that she did not intend to become a fashion trendsetter.

After he became president, the notoriously tone-deaf Grant was obliged to attend concerts and musical performances. He manfully endured them, and after one was asked how he had enjoyed the evening. Not a man to dissemble, he replied, "How could I? I know only two tunes: one of them is 'Yankee Doodle,' and the other isn't."

Grant had little political experience, so he left much of the daily administration to his cabinet, the collection of friends and party officials who had helped get him elected. Ironically, they perpetrated so many frauds that Grant's government is remembered mostly for the extent of its corruption, although it is only too clear that the president himself did not benefit from it. He left office almost penniless and instantly embarked on writing his memoirs, for which he received an advance of $50,000.

heavy politics

William Taft (1857–1930) was a reluctant candidate for the Republican nomination in 1908, saying, "Politics makes me sick. I would much prefer to go onto the Supreme Bench for life than to run for the presidency." Taft was spurred on by the encouragement of President Theodore Roosevelt, and more especially by his wife Nellie, who had said when she was 17 that she wanted to be married to the President of the United States some day. In 1921, Taft realized his own ambition when he was appointed Chief Justice of the Supreme Court.

Taft still holds the record as the heaviest president to occupy the Oval Office (1909–1913). Standing 6 ft, 2 in. tall and weighing a stately 350 pounds, he was unfailingly polite, and always rose from his seat on a streetcar to offer it, as wags said, to the nearest three ladies. On arrival at the White House, he discovered that some of the facilities were inadequate for his needs, not least the bathtub, in which he got stuck. He had it replaced with an extra-large one, which could accommodate four average-sized people.

Shortly after his election he decided to spend his summers in the small Massachusetts town of Beverly to escape the heat and humidity of Washington. Once established in what became known as the "Summer White House," Taft could combine administration with relaxation and was a keen swimmer. One day, when he was swimming off the Massachusetts coast, a young couple wondered whether they too could take a dip in the ocean. The young lady hesitated, saying, "Perhaps we had better wait a moment—the president is using the ocean at the moment."

life at the zoo

Devotees of *The West Wing* on TV may think they are reasonably familiar with the interior of the White House, but its hallowed corridors once rang to the sound of children shouting and playing boisterously. When Theodore Roosevelt became president in 1901, he arrived with his wife, six children, and a menagerie of pets. Roosevelt had the West Wing constructed so that he could work in peace, which seems to have been in short supply among his lively family. Ike Hoover, a White House servant, recalled in his memoirs that "the house became one general playground for them...no furniture too good or too high to use for leapfrog and horseplay, no bed too expensive or chair too elegantly upholstered to be used as a resting place for the various pets of the household." When they left, Roosevelt remarked, "I don't think any family has enjoyed the White House more than we have,"—but then he wasn't one of the long-suffering staff members who had to put up with the children clattering over the precious furnishings on stilts, nor did he have to clean up after the pony that was given elevator rides, or cover the bicycle tracks on the carpets.

Roosevelt's daughter Alice, who went on to become a noted society hostess, managed to scandalize Washington society and annoy the politicians with her habit of wandering in and out of the Oval Office while her father was in conference. When they complained to the president, he replied in exasperation, "I can be president of the United States, or I can control Alice. I cannot possibly do both."

name dRoPPeR

Politicians are not always accorded the respect they think they deserve. When Teddy Roosevelt was President McKinley's vice-president (1901–1909) he was caught in a fire at a hotel. After the fire had been put out, the guests were forced to hang around rather aimlessly. Roosevelt wanted to get back to his room, and protested to the hotel manager, "But I'm the vice-president." His words had the desired effect, and Roosevelt was allowed back inside. Just as he reached the stairs, the manager called out, "Wait a minute! What are you vice-president of?" "Why the United States of course," Roosevelt replied. "Then get the hell back down here," the manager shouted. "I though you were vice-president of the hotel!"

worn-out machinery

Woodrow Wilson (1856–1924) was one of only three presidents to marry while in office. A widower himself, he met the widow Edith Bolling Galt at a White House reception in 1915 and married her a mere nine months later. In an inadvertent admission about their pre-marital relationship, Edith later recalled that she was rather stunned by Woodrow's proposal of marriage and said, "I was so surprised that I nearly fell out of bed."

In 1919 President Wilson collapsed with a stoke that paralyzed his left side and impaired his vision. He was almost completely incapacitated, but he neither resigned from office, nor passed the burden of his duties to the vice-president. Instead, his wife and his physician successfully hid the extent of his illness from the American people and Edith Wilson, who was later called the first woman president, began a period of "stewardship" for the remaining 17 months of his presidency. When Wilson finally died in 1924, he said, "The machinery is just worn out. I am ready."

bad boy harding

Warren G. Harding's presidency (1921–1923) was tainted by scandal partly because he invited his cronies to the White House for regular evenings of carousing, drinking, and gambling in spite of the Prohibition laws. His advisors were known as the "Poker Cabinet," and on one occasion when the president was down on his luck he gambled away some White House china. After his death it emerged that this was the least of his crimes, as the "Teapot Dome" scandal erupted, which involved the bribery of officials over oil reserves in Teapot Dome, Wyoming. Harding himself once presciently observed, "I known how far removed from greatness I am."

silent cal

Calvin Coolidge, the 30th US president, was a man of integrity but was not one of the most extrovert presidents. Known as "Silent Cal" for his famously brief statements to the press, Coolidge's reputation as a man of few words was well known. One evening at dinner, a woman turned to him saying, "I have made a bet, Mr. Coolidge, that I can get more than two words out of you." "You lose," replied the president, who concentrated on eating for the rest of the meal.

The inauguration address of Coolidge was the first to be broadcast on the radio. Ironically, 23 million people heard "Silent Cal," the quiet man of American politics.

Coolidge obviously had an air of gravitas that may have intimidated those around him. Something of a control freak, he supervised the minutest domestic details of the White House, from the menus to the housekeeping plans. His wife Grace was noted for her charm and easy manners and was seen as a contrast to her taciturn husband. At one White House garden party, she had been instructed not to speak to the press, but responded to reporter's questions in sign language—Grace had taught deaf children before her arrival in Washington.

One Sunday, Calvin went to church alone because Grace was unwell, and when he returned she asked him about the sermon. Calvin told her that the preacher had spoken about sin, but his wife wanted to know more and asked her husband exactly what he had said. "He was against it," the president replied.

When Coolidge's death was announced in 1933, Dorothy Parker exclaimed, "How can they tell?"

the presidency

hoover antics

Even presidents are flattered when asked for their autographs, but President Herbert Hoover couldn't quite understand why one collector wanted three copies of his signature. He later found out that the recipient intended to keep one and trade the other two—the going rate was two Hoovers for one Babe Ruth (the baseball star).

Although President Rutherford B. Hayes installed the first telephone in the White House and was instructed in its use by none other than Alexander Graham Bell, Hoover was the first president to enjoy the luxury of a private telephone line in the Oval Office. Until his presidency (1929–1933), the president had to use the phone in the White House hallway.

Hoover graduated as a mining engineer and made his fortune working around the world. By the time he was 40, he was a multimillionaire and decided to devote his life to politics. He served two presidents as Commerce Secretary before being elected president in 1929, but for the duration of his 47-year-career as a public servant, he donated all of his paychecks to charity.

history bites

trouble with the mrs.

F.D.R. Roosevelt was the first president to appoint a woman to a cabinet post. His wife, the formidable Eleanor Roosevelt, was a strong supporter of women's rights but understood how tricky the decision must have been for her husband. She asked him if the labor leaders had objected to the decision. "Oh that's alright," he replied. "I'd rather have trouble with them for an hour than trouble with you for the rest of my life."

When Roosevelt died on April 12, 1945, his vice-president Harry S. Truman was ushered into his sitting room where the news was broken to him. "Is there anything I can do for you?" Truman asked FDR's widow, Eleanor. "Is there anything *we* can do for *you*? Eleanor replied. "You're the one in trouble now!"

The next day the new President Truman, obviously overwhelmed by events, remarked to reporters, "Boys if you ever pray, pray for me now. I don't know if you fellows ever had a load of hay fall on you, but when they told me yesterday what had happened, I felt like the moon, the stars, and all the planets had fallen on me."

the Presidency

beating the headlines

Truman ran for re-election in 1948 against the New York senator Thomas Dewey. A faltering economy had contributed to a decline in Truman's popularity but Dewey was not the most inspiring of candidates, either. Famous for stating the obvious, Dewey once told an audience, "You know your future is still ahead of you."

The outcome was close but pollsters firmly believed that Dewey would win. Accordingly, many newspapers went to press before the election results were announced, having printed their front pages based on the pollsters' predictions: "Dewey defeats Truman." The real result was encapsulated in one picture on the following day, which showed a delighted Harry Truman, secure in the White House, holding up the erroneous headline in the *Chicago Tribune*.

never too old to fight

Dwight D. Eisenhower (1890–1969), the only president to fight in both World Wars, wanted to join the navy, but at the age of 20 was deemed too old, so he signed up at West Point instead. His mother was a pacifist and cried when she heard that he had embarked on a military career.

history bites

Ronald Duck

Superstitious commentators have noted that since 1840, all American presidents elected in a year ending in zero have died in office. The exception to this was Ronald Reagan, although he survived an assassination attempt in 1981 (and so far, George W. Bush has been spared). Reagan suffered a chest wound, and as he was wheeled into the operating theater, he quipped to the surgeons, "I hope you're all Republicans." Turning to his wife Nancy, the 70-year-old president tried to cheer her up by saying, "Sorry honey. I forgot to duck."

Colorful Past

Most men elected to the dignity of the office of president of the United States have succeeded in conducting themselves with the decorum befitting their position. Not all enjoyed entirely blameless careers before their arrival in the Oval Office, however. Andrew Jackson actually killed a man in a duel in 1806, shooting Charles Dickinson dead after he had been hit in the ribs himself. Jackson survived this incident only to be the subject of an assassination attempt in 1835 when a disgruntled house painter fired two pistols at him at point-blank range. Fortunately, both misfired, although the

67-year-old president, nicknamed "Old Hickory," showed no fear and attempted to throttle his assailant with his walking cane.

Theodore Roosevelt was another president who had enjoyed a colorful past before settling down to politics. After the deaths of both his wife and mother in the same year, Roosevelt worked on a cattle ranch in the wild North Dakota Territory in 1884. Physically, he was not a natural rancher, being small and bespectacled, and when he was taunted as "four-eyes" in a bar one night, Roosevelt responded by punching the drunken cowhand, who struck his head on the bar as he went down and passed out. Roosevelt returned to his dinner.

Even when he was president, Roosevelt continued to spar as exercise, although was forced to stop when a heavy punch damaged the sight in his left eye.

Roosevelt was also the subject of an assassination attempt in 1912 after he had left office, when a deranged man shot him. John Schrank had apparently been told in a dream that Roosevelt was responsible for the death of President McKinley. Roosevelt was wounded, but was saved from serious injury by his spectacle case and the folds of a 50-page speech. He insisted on continuing with his speech in Milwaukee, saying, "I will make this speech or die."

When Harry Truman confronted a similar assassination threat in 1950, he responded phlegmatically: "A president has to expect these things."

history bites

ghostly presidents

The White House is apparently haunted by a number of ghosts, the most distinguished being that of Abraham Lincoln. Eleanor Roosevelt reported in her memoirs that one of the maids once burst into her room in an agitated state, shrieking, "He's up there—sitting on the edge of the bed, taking off his shoes!" When Mrs Roosevelt asked whom she meant, the maid replied "Mr. Lincoln"—who had been dead for 75 years.

Adlai Stevenson stayed in the bedroom in 1952, only too aware of the ghostly stories surrounding the room. He found that he was too overwrought to sleep and wandered around the room looking at all the historic artifacts. When he finally went to sleep, he couldn't bring himself to sleep on Lincoln's bed and dozed off on the sofa instead. The next day, he discovered that the bed was not Lincoln's, but the sofa was.

President Reagan's daughter Maureen had a dog, which used to stand outside the empty Lincoln Bedroom barking at the door, and always refused to go in.

over-protection

The security surrounding the president increases with every passing year and the work of the close protection unit sometimes attracts adverse attention. Every venue that the president visits is checked in advance by the secret service and placed under close surveillance until the leader of the free world leaves. When President Eisenhower planned to see a performance of *La Bohème* in Washington, the opera impresario Rudolf Bing was interviewed by the security services. "We hear the girl dies," one of the agents began. "How is she killed?" "She dies of consumption," Bing replied, before adding wickedly (and with a straight face), "But it isn't catching at a distance."

mission impossible

Richard Nixon, the only US President to resign from office in the face of impeachment, enjoyed a roller-coaster political career. He was highly intelligent and an instinctive politician; "No one," he said in 1990, "had ever been so high and fallen so low." When he was growing up his mother hoped he would become a Quaker missionary.

tramps and hot dogs

When President Ford entertained Queen Elizabeth II in America's bicentennial year, he was aware of the great honor, and realized that it was a time for America to try to recover its dignity in the wake of

Nixon's disgrace and the Watergate affair. It is perhaps a shame that when he escorted the queen on to the dance floor, the orchestra struck up "The Lady is a Tramp."

The British royal family may have been prepared for unusual situations at the White House, however. Fifty years earlier, Eleanor Roosevelt attracted vocal criticism from Americans because she served hot dogs to King George VI and Queen Elizabeth.

POLITICAL AFFAIRS

SERVING A PURPOSE

In 1282, the Welsh prince Llewellyn ap Gruffud died after defeat in battle by Edward I of England. After centuries of dispute, Wales was finally annexed to England. Aware of the need to appease the suspicious Welsh populace, however, Edward promised to provide them with a new prince, and promised one who spoke no English. Two years later, Edward was true to his word and invited the Welsh nobility to Caernarvon Castle to meet their new lord—his two-day-old son, Prince Edward. The king held the young prince in his arms and shouted in Welsh, *Eich dyn* ("This is your man"), which may explain the origin of the Prince of Wales' motto, *Ich dien,* or "I serve."

beheading the scottish queen

Elizabeth I (1533–1603) imprisoned her cousin Mary, Queen of Scots (1542–1587) for 20 years and during this time the Scottish queen remained the focus for Catholic plotters against Elizabeth. Finally, after the discovery of the Babington Plot against the English queen's life in 1586, Mary was tried and found guilty of treason. After many months of vacillation, Elizabeth signed Mary's death warrant, which she then ripped up before it could be dispatched. Some days later, the Queen was persuaded to sign another death warrant, which Lord Burghley immediately sent to Mary's jailers. When Elizabeth received news of the Scottish queen's execution five days later, she reacted with very public rage and horror, blaming her councilors for sending off the warrant without her permission. Furious, she sent her secretary to the Tower and wrote almost apologetically to Mary's son, James VI of Scotland about "the extreme dolor that overwhelms my mind for that miserable accident which (far contrary to my meaning) hath befallen." It seems she was trying to avoid responsibility and blame her staff.

The Elizabethan court (and indeed most others) was a place of very formal and regimented manners. Woe betides the courtier who did not know his or her place or who offended the monarch by inappropriate behavior. Ambitious nobles knew that their first royal introduction was critically important, as the monarch's first impression of a courtier was often lasting. In the words of the diarist John Aubrey, the unfortunate Edward de Vere, the 17th Earl of Oxford and a noted poet "making his low obeisance to Queen Elizabeth, happened to let a fart, at which he was so abashed and ashamed that he went to travel for seven years. On his return the Queen welcomed him home, and said 'My lord, I had forgotten the Fart.'"

POLITICAL AFFAIRS

Ranting On

English politics in the middle years of the 17th century was populated by a number of quaintly named sects: Levellers, Ranters, Clubmen, Diggers, and Engagers all vied to influence the course of events during the Civil War. One of the less significant groups were the Ranters, who reacted against the restraint of the Puritans by encouraging free love, smoking, and swearing as a means to spiritual salvation. Not surprisingly, the Puritan-dominated Parliament passed the Adultery Act, swiftly followed by the Blasphemy Act in 1650 in an attempt to stop their excesses. Many Ranters were imprisoned and Jacob Bauthumley, who was convicted of writing a blasphemous treatise, had a hole bored in his tongue.

Neutral Club

The Clubmen were small local associations who struggled to maintain some sort of neutrality during the war years, and more importantly, keep the fighting away from their localities. There were spontaneous uprisings of Clubmen in the mid-1640s that were really demonstrations by a war-weary populace. Poorly trained and ill-equipped, the Clubmen did not present much of a threat and Cromwell dismissed them as "poor, silly creatures, whom if you please to let me send them home, they promise to be very dutiful."

history bites

air tax

The Protestant ascendancy was established in Ireland in the 17th century and was far from universally popular among the native Catholic population. The Irish rightly believed that the English exploited Ireland and the Irish for their own economic gain. The Anglo-Irish clergyman and satirist Jonathan Swift (1667–1745) was both a part of the English regime and also keen to criticize it. When Lady Carteret, the viceroy's wife commented on the excellent quality of the air in Ireland, Swift replied, "For God's sake, madam, don't say that in England, for if you do, they will surely tax it!"

wig tax

When Louis XIII (1601–1643) adopted a wig to cover up his premature baldness in 1624, he began a trend for wig wearing that lasted almost 200 years. Men of the aristocracy and bourgeoisie copied the monarch so that, by the turn of the 17th century, anyone who had pretensions to fashion wore a wig. They were incredibly expensive, costing about the same as a whole outfit of clothes, and they were made from horsehair, yak hair, or human hair. Wigs required a get deal of care, especially when it became fashionable to color them with powder from about 1715. As the 18th century wore on, wigs for both men and women became ever more elaborate until the prime minister William Pitt imposed an extraordinary tax. As part of his perpetual effort to raise money for the wars against France, Pitt taxed wig powder, which had the almost immediate effect of ending the fashion for wigs, powdered and otherwise. After the Terror of 1793, the popularity of wigs declined even more rapidly in France because they were associated with the despised aristocracy.

COLBERT'S TAX

The French statesman Jean Baptiste Colbert (1619–1683) is credited with revolutionizing the French financial system. Louis XIV's chief finance minister, Colbert banished corruption, made the collection of taxes more efficient, and doubled the revenue of the state in the space of ten years. He worked very hard and trode a fine line between raising revenues and not antagonizing the public, saying: "The art of taxation consists in so plucking the goose as to obtain the largest amount of feathers with the least amount of hissing."

BOSTON TEA PARTY

In 1773, many of George III's subjects in North America were becoming increasingly disgruntled by the imposition of taxes from a distant government. The Boston Tea Party was one of the most famous instances of their rebellion before the outbreak of full-scale war. It is well known that a group of men dressed as Indians boarded the tea ships in Boston harbor and tipped the cargo of tea into the sea. What is less well known is that the colonists were utterly determined that no one (especially not the British) should be able to use one leaf of the tea, and as one participant, George Hewes reported, "...The next morning, after we had cleared the ships of the tea, it was discovered that very considerable quantities of it were floating upon the surface of the water; and to prevent the possibility of any of its being saved for use, a number of small boats were manned by sailors and citizens, who rowed them into those parts of the harbor wherever the tea was visible, and by beating it with oars and paddles so thoroughly drenched it as to render its entire destruction inevitable."

Last-minute Replacement

Thomas Jefferson, famous as the architect of the Declaration of the Independence, was only summoned to the Second Continental Congress at the last minute as a replacement for one Peyton Randolph who had been called home to Virginia. At 33, Jefferson was the second-youngest delegate and his reputation rested on one tract, the *Summary View of the Rights of British America*, written two years earlier. He was regarded as a dilettante and was rather reluctant to take part in the whole process. "During the whole time I sat with him I never heard him utter three sentences together," John Adams recalled later.

hanging around

The statesman Benjamin Franklin (1706–1790) was only too aware of the enormity of the steps the Continental Congress was taking in 1776. Before the signing of the Declaration of Independence, he urged his arguing colleagues to remain united: "We must, indeed, all hang together, or most assuredly we shall all hang separately."

getting along

Drafting the constitution of the new nation occupied the members of the Pennsylvania Assembly for some three months in 1776, as delegates debated and argued about the constituent points. During that period, American citizens somehow coped with the legal limbo of the country by carrying on as normal, going about their daily business as usual. The observant Benjamin Franklin noticed and tried to impress on his colleagues the need for speed with his usual trenchant eloquence. "Gentlemen you see we have been living under anarchy, yet the business of living has gone on as usual. Be careful; if our debates go on too much longer, people may come to see that they can get along very well without us!"

history bites

date mix up

The fourth of July is celebrated as Independence Day in the United States, and recalls the signing of the Declaration of Independence, but the parties and barbeques should really be held on July 2. The colonists agreed to declare independence from Great Britain on July 2 and the proposal was not actually signed until August 2, after it had been transcribed on to parchment. On July 4 the president of the proceedings, John Hancock, and his secretary simply signed the announcement of the form of words that were to be used. All the delegates to the Continental Congress were expected to sign the actual declaration and the last didn't put his name to it until 1781. John Adams was almost right when he wrote his wife Abigail that "the second day of July, 1776, will be the most memorable Epocha in the History of America."

new monarchy

In 1776, having swept aside the rule of Great Britain, the colonists considered establishing a monarchy for the newly formed United States. It is worth remembering that the Declaration of Independence takes issue only with George III, the "present king of Great Britain," and, in addition, the concept of government by the people for the people was a radical one that had yet to be embraced. So the second son of George III, Frederick, Duke of York was briefly considered, until the idea of a republic headed by a president stuck fast.

Funnily enough, Oliver Cromwell was offered the throne in 1657 after few years as Lord Protector of England, and probably the only reason he was never crowned is that he died before he was able to act on the proposal.

The loss of the 13 colonies was a severe blow to George III's prestige and went on to haunt his successors. Over 150 years later his great-granddaughter, Queen Mary was heard to remark to an American officer during World War II, "Perhaps we should still be one country if my great-grandfather hadn't been so obstinate."

Whisky tax

One of the most memorable demands of the 13 colonies was "No taxation without representation." Only 15 years later, the United States government imposed a Whisky Tax on the nation that so enraged the people of Western Pennsylvania that they revolted against it. The frontiersmen regarded it as yet another tax imposed on honest farmers by the Easterners and government collectors were attacked; one inspector was even tarred and feathered by irate citizens. President Washington sent an army of 12,000 men to put down the Whisky Rebellion, but failed to see the irony of the situation: the new

American government was imposing an arbitrary and unpopular tax on the people in exactly the same way as the British had earlier in the century.

saved by a scarf

Once secure as First Consul of France, Napoleon Bonaparte was the subject of several assassination attempts as his rivals, both Royalist and Jacobin, tried to remove him from power. In 1800, he was saved from death by the fact that the Empress Josephine delayed his departure for the opera because she couldn't decide which scarf to wear. Eventually, two coaches set out, the emperor in the first, and the empress and her daughter in the second. In an effort to make up for lost time, Napoleon's coachman drove fast through the Paris streets, and hurtled past the conspirators' bomb (which became known as the "Infernal Device") seconds before it detonated. Fortunately Josephine's carriage was far enough behind to avoid the full force of the explosion, although it destroyed several buildings and killed or injured some 52 people.

Napoleon arrived at his final place of exile during the night of October 17, 1815. He stayed the first night on the remote Atlantic outpost of St. Helena in bed and breakfast accommodation and by the strangest of coincidences his landlord, a Mr. Porteous, had let the same room to the Duke of Wellington only a few months earlier.

Wellington wrote from Napoleon's former palace in Paris, "You may tell Bony, that I find his apartments at the Elissé Bourbon very convenient and that I hope he likes mine ... It is a droll sequel enough to the affairs of Europe that we should change places of residence."

Talking Bunk

The scholar and Congregationalist minister William Jenks (1778–1866) was a respected Massachusetts humanitarian and man of letters. In 1808, aware of growing tensions in the new American nation, he made what has turned out to be an uncanny prediction about the future of the young nation. "The northern states will fight the southern states and the fight will be about slavery...the northern states will defeat the exhausted southern states in a war that lasted four years...After the war we will have a new United States of America." He set the date for this conflagration as 1856, which is when the trouble began brewing with John Brown at Harper's Ferry.

Predictable Strife

Politicians' reputations depend not only on their beliefs and promises to the electorate, but also on their charisma and eloquence. In December 1819, Felix Walker, the veteran Congressional representative for Buncombe North Carolina, made a long and

history bites

tedious speech just at the point when other members in the House of Representatives wanted to wrap up the debate on the Missouri Question. Walker replied loftily that he was not addressing the house and indeed said that members did not even need to listen to his words because, he said, "I'm talking to Buncombe." Congressmen adopted the word "Buncombe" as slang for nonsense (dull and otherwise) and as the word gained wider dissemination, it became shortened to bunk.

dixieland

The southern states of the USA are often referred to as "Dixieland," which is a reference to colonial times when France was the ruling power. The name derives from the fact that when banks were permitted to issue their own paper money in the early years of the 19th century, one bank in New Orleans printed $10 bills with the word French word *dix* (10) on the back. The notes duly became known as "Dixies," and the term Dixieland became more widely known after a song entitled "Dixie's Land' became popular after 1859.

beer love

The Know Nothing Party was one of the more obscure political
parties of 19th-century America, but in 1855 the mayor of Chicago,
Dr. Levi Boone, followed the party's largely anti-immigrant policies.
He took against the city's German population, targeting in particular
their very un-American habit of beer drinking on Sunday afternoons,
which they tended to do in the company of the Irish, an even more
despised group. When Boone raised liquor license fees by 500
percent and prohibited the sale of alcohol on Sundays, his laws were
largely ignored. The police proceeded to arrest more than 200
German beer drinkers (ignoring native Chicagoans who broke the
law) and on the day of their trial, an armed mob of 300 tackled the
mayor's policemen. Terrified of the mob, Boone was forced by the
Chicago Beer rioters to back down. His party was discredited and
Chicago went on to become one of the great beer cities of America.
The mayor should have remembered the words of Benjamin Franklin:
"Beer is proof that God loves us and wants us to be happy."

war between the states

In 1861, Europeans watched with a mixture of horror and
bemusement as the War Between the States unfolded, but it was
summed up irreverently by the writer and historian Thomas Carlyle

(1795–1881). They are, he said, "cutting each other's throats because one half of them prefer hiring their servants for life, and the other by the hour."

weight in bacon

Carlyle's reputation as the "Sage of Chelsea" was established in 1837 with the publication of the magisterial *History of the French Revolution.* The work would have appeared earlier, except that the philosopher John Stuart Mill had accidentally used the manuscript of the first volume to light a fire. Carlyle had no choice except to laboriously rewrite the whole thing.

In 1875, Carlyle was delighted to be offered a knighthood by Queen Victoria, but declined it. He knew that the moving force behind the offer was the Prime Minister, Benjamin Disraeli, a man he had despised, although belatedly felt he had misjudged. However, a few years later, when he disagreed with government policy on foreign affairs, he forgot how delighted he had been with Disraeli's offer and referred to the prime minister as "a cursed old Jew, not worth his weight in bacon."

decorating the carpet

At the height of his success, Charles Dickens visited America, where he was lionized and introduced to the highest in the land. He published details of his tour in *American Notes,* where he reported on some of the differences between various aspects of life in Britain and America. The habit of chewing tobacco and spitting the excess juice into a spittoon was not simply limited to frontiersmen, he wrote, but was also practiced by the nation's politicians in Congress. Dickens noticed that Congress itself was "handsomely carpeted; but the state to which these carpets are reduced by the universal disregard of the spittoon with which every honorable member is accommodated, and the extraordinary improvements on the pattern which are squirted and dabbled upon it in every direction, do not admit to being described."

President Andrew Jackson was responsible for buying 20 spittoons for the East Room of the White House at a cost of $12.50 each. The purchase was not without controversy: opponents dubbed it a great waste of public money, while supporters pointed out that they would help preserve the White House carpets.

history bites

Lending a hand

The Suez Canal was opened in 1869, the culmination of a great project largely financed by the French and engineered by the diplomat Ferdinand de Lesseps (1805–1894). For the British with the empire in India, it was of great practical and strategic importance as it cut the three-month journey time to India down to just a month. When the Khedive of Egypt wanted to sell his shares in 1875, the British government under Benjamin Disraeli was determined that they should not go to the French. There was simply the minor problem of finding the money to buy them. Parliament was not sitting so the prime minister was unable to raise the funds through the usual channels and was forced to turn to private investors. Fortunately, Baron Rothschild reacted coolly when Disraeli asked for a £4 million loan.

"When do you want it?" asked Rothschild.

"Tomorrow" replied Disraeli.

"What is your security?" enquired Rothschild.

"The British government," replied the flamboyant prime minister.

The reply seemed to satisfy Rothschild, who authorized the transfer and enabled Disraeli to pull off a diplomatic coup.

POLITICAL AFFAIRS

getting on with the neighbors

In the early years of the 20th century, the French ambassador, Jean Jusserand found himself discussing pacifism with the First Lady Edith Roosevelt who urged him to consider the example of Canada and the United States. "We have a 3,000-mile unfortified frontier. You people arm yourselves to the teeth," she said reprovingly. Perhaps Mrs. Roosevelt had forgotten the troubled history of relations between France and Germany, but Jusserand just replied wistfully, "Ah Madame, perhaps we could exchange neighbors."

In 1916, while negotiating what became the Balfour Declaration, which laid out plans for the establishment of a Jewish state in Palestine, Chaim Weizmann, later the first Israeli president, tried to explain the Jewish attachment to the land of Palestine. "Just suppose I were to offer you Paris instead of London. Would you accept it?" asked Weizmann. Balfour struggled to comprehend the whole concept, replying in bewilderment, "We already have London." "We had Jerusalem," Weizmann replied, "when London was a marsh."

italian chic

During the negotiations that produced the Treaty of Versailles at the end of the World War I, President Woodrow Wilson opposed the Italian annexation of the Adriatic port of Fiume, a town that had previously been part of the Austro-Hungarian Empire. The Italians tried to convince the president that the town's culture, population, and language were all Italian, and so the transfer was a logical move. Wilson thought for a moment, before replying, "I hope you won't press the point in respect to New York City, or you might feel like claiming a sizeable piece of Manhattan Island."

what a type

Adolf Hitler was not always the easiest man to get along with and understandably, his staff were loathe to upset the Führer. Given to explosive outbursts of temper, Hitler was also slightly vain and refused to wear the glasses he needed for reading, insisting instead that all documents for his attention should be produced in really large type. The only way to accommodate this order was to produce a completely new typewriter which featured extra large keys and was known as the Führer typewriter. During World War II in Germany, it was also illegal to name a horse Adolf.

communist priest

One of the most feared dictators of the 20th century and the man responsible for the deaths of millions of Russians was nearly a priest. Between 1894 and 1899 Joseph Stalin (1879–1953) studied at a

Russian theological seminary in Tiflis, Georgia, but he was later expelled when he became a Marxist and joined the Social Democrat Party.

POWER STRUGGLE

Stalin carefully built up his power base so that he was able to sweep to power on the death of Lenin in 1924. His enemies or perceived opponents were ruthlessly purged and it is estimated that some ten million people were killed or simply disappeared in 1932–1933 alone. His inner circle understood that they were especially vulnerable to the dictator's whims, but when in the middle of an especially bitter debate, Stalin suddenly collapsed, Beria the chief of police couldn't help himself. Viewing the recumbent Soviet leader, lying apparently dead on the floor, Beria leaped to his feet shouting, "We're free at last." Stalin's daughter Svetlana raced into the room and took her father's hand. The old man miraculously opened his eyes, fixing them on a petrified Beria, who dropped to his knees.

Stalin once stated: "A single death is a tragedy. A million deaths is a statistic."

When Stalin died in 1953 the wily, Machiavellian Nikita Khrushchev (1894–1971) filled the power vacuum at the center of Soviet politics. Virtually illiterate until the age of 25, Khrushchev peppered his pronouncements with salty peasant humor and language. Khrushchev denounced Stalin's reign of terror in 1956 and did much to improve the reputation of he Soviet Union during his 11-year rule. "Politicians are the same all over," he once said. "They promise to build a bridge even where there is no river."

WAX LYRICAL

The cult of personality is what helps keep many dictators in power, and in some cases it lasts long after their death. Probably the most famous case is that of the Soviet Union's first leader, V. I. Lenin, who died in 1924. Revered as the founder of the Soviet state, Lenin's demise devastated the nation and on the day of his death alone, the government received over 100 pleas that his body should be preserved for the benefit of future generations. Two days after his death Russia's most prominent pathologist meticulously embalmed the body and a tomb was erected by the Kremlin Wall in Moscow's Red Square. Between 1924 and 1972, 73 million people filed past Lenin's body, which was removed once a year to be "rejuvenated." Today, the corpse looks suspiciously waxy, but neither the Soviet authorities nor the current regime were or are willing to discuss the body's authenticity.

Political Affairs

Cuban Survival

Fidel Castro has ruled Cuba as an independent Communist state for over 40 years, despite the best efforts of the country's closest neighbor, the USA. In 1978, Castro estimated that he had survived some 60 assassination attempts, which ranged from poisoned milkshakes, botched bombs that missed their target, but melted Havana's traffic lights, and even poisoned cold cream. Finally, a trained assassin was found, but she admitted she was a huge admirer of Fidel and would rather cook him a hearty meal than shoot him.

Cheese Eaters

The French are often defined by their gastronomy and not always in a flattering way: the nation was recently vilified as "cheese-eating surrender monkeys," by a high-ranking U.S. official. In the early 1960s, the most famous French president, Charles de Gaulle, was beset by a seemingly unending string of political crises and was heard to groan, "How can one possible govern a country that has over 350 kinds of cheese?"

history bites

Wacky tax

Governments are often extremely inventive when it comes to devising new ways of taxing their populations. Nothing is exempt and over the centuries, windows, hearths, blueberries, and wigs are just some of the items that have been liable. In several U.S. states, illegal drugs are taxed. In a bizarre maneuver, drug users can pay the tax at their local Department of Revenue, but will not be prosecuted by the revenue officers for illicit drug use. North Carolina reports that since the tax was imposed in 1990, only 77 people have come forward to pay it.

CRime and PunishmenT

show some RespecT

The first recorded laws in human history survive from the Mesopotamian civilization. King Urukagina, who reigned during the 24th century BC and was married to Queen Shagshag, drew up the first judicial code to combat corruption.

Hamurrabi's Code, which dates from *c.* 1780 BC, survives on a stone slab and laid out many laws familiar to Christians from the Bible. Another Mesopotamian king, Hamurrabi stressed that the punishment must fit the crime and laid out the basic legal principle of "an eye for an eye." Punishments for offences we may regard as reasonably trivial, such as stealing, were punishable by death. Nuns who were caught visiting taverns were burnt to death, and tavern-keepers guilty of overcharging customers were to be thrown into the nearest river (and presumably left to drown). Shoddy builders are also warned: "If a builder builds a house for someone and does not construct it properly and the house which he built falls in and kills its owner, then that builder shall be put to death."

Domestic arguments were covered in some detail, with penalties ranging from impalement to fines, depending on the offense; women found guilty of neglecting their husbands were sentenced to being "cast into the water." Finally, respect for parents was rigorously encouraged: sons who hit their fathers were to have their hands cut off.

coat burial

The first written law code in ancient Greece emerged in about 620 BC, when the politician Draco sought to end the confusion and violence of law by vendetta. Draco's law code was undoubtedly harsh—and it is from his name that the word Draconian comes—but it did provide a uniform system of laws. The death penalty was advocated for inconsequential offenses, but the severe punishments certainly deterred criminals. Draco's law was received with great popular acclaim and when he had finished reading it out to the people of Athens, they showed their appreciation in the traditional manner by showering him with coats, hats, and cloaks, burying him completely. When he was dug out, Draco was dead, having been suffocated by the bombardment of apparel.

CRIME AND PUNISHMENT

Oiling the Wheels

Tax collectors in ancient Egypt were known as scribes and were empowered to enter people's homes and check over their property. In one era a tax was imposed on cooking oil, which was issued in set amounts to every household. The scribes not only issued the oil, but they also checked that the appropriate amount was consumed and that householders were not illicitly re-using oil to cook foods and thus avoiding buying new oil.

Wee Tax

The Roman Emperor Vespasian (AD 9–79) was a great reformer who reorganized the Roman army, built the Coliseum, and improved the financial security of Rome by taxing a diverse selection of commodities. He is possibly the only ruler in history to impose a tax on the use of urinals, a tax that his son Titus believed was highly undignified. Vespasian was more pragmatic, and pointed out that money was money, wherever it came from. He held up a handful of coins to his son's nose and said, "See? They do not smell."

Naked Protection

The Holy Roman Emperor Charlemagne (747–814) was the first great lawgiver of the early Middle Ages and inherited law codes from both the Romans and Germanic tribes. Although the status of women in this period placed them in a lower social and economic position than men, they were at least protected by the law. The laws of the Germanic Alamanni tribe fined a man 60 sous for stealing the headdress of a woman while she was out walking, while under the Lombard legal code, a man could be put to death for stealing a woman's clothes while she was bathing. The form of death was far more prolonged and painful if the unfortunate woman was forced to walk home naked.

a king's ransom

Richard I (1157–99) departed on Crusade a mere three months after his coronation, leaving his sizeable realm in the control of the barons and his brother John. In fact, Richard spent only six months of his ten-year reign in England, reappearing only to raise money for his foreign exploits. Taxes such as the "Saladin Tithe" of 1188 were wildly unpopular: "Every one shall give in alms for this year's aid of the land of Jerusalem a tenth of his rents and movables." His crusading was not an unqualified success and he fell out with his fellow crusaders, King Philip Augustus of France and Raymond, Count of Toulouse. It was because of this latter disagreement that Richard had to travel home in disguise—had he journeyed through France he would probably have been imprisoned. In the event, Duke

CRIME AND PUNISHMENT

Leopold of Austria captured the king in 1193 and ransomed him for the prodigious sum of 150,000 marks. One chronicler in England recorded gloomily, "In order to secure his release, every man in England was required to contribute one-fourth of his income and every sheep was shorn."

MERCILESS CARPET

The Venetian explorer Marco Polo (1254–1324) reported on the customs and laws of the Mongol people under Kublai Khan. One particularly strict law forbad the spilling of royal blood on the ground, so when Kublai Khan defeated his uncle Nyan, he had him put to death in an ingenious method and at the same time, made sure that virtually no one knew about it. "He commanded that he should be put to death straightaway and in secret, lest endeavors should be made to obtain pity and pardon for him...he was wrapt in a carpet and tossed to and fro mercilessly until he died."

RATS!

Legal cases against animals were not uncommon in medieval times. In 1445 a group of beetles was summoned to appear before French justices, charged with destroying crops. The case was abandoned because the beetles ignored the summons. In another ridiculous case in 1500, rats were charged with trespass for infesting people's homes. The defense lawyer played for time, arguing that the entire rat population of the village should be summoned. When they failed to appear after three writs, he said they were prepared to come to court, but were afraid of reprisals from local cats.

it's a dog's life

As recently as 1924, a dog was sentenced to life imprisonment in Pike County, Pennsylvania for killing a cat. When a circus elephant ran amok in Tennessee in 1916 and injured its trainer, it was not killed outright, but was awarded a fair trial before being sentenced to death by hanging.

From medieval times until the early 18th century, many countries passed sumptuary laws that imposed rules on the clothing worn by various ranks of society. Some of the laws existed simply to define rank, and others were imposed in an attempt to boost trade. In 17th-century New Jersey, women were forbidden to use any artificial aids to improve their appearance, in case they managed to lure innocent men into matrimony under false pretences. The authorities were so worried about the possibility of women conning men into marriage, that they imposed the same strict punishments as those for crimes of witchcraft and sorcery. "Be it resolved that all women, of whatever age, rank, profession, or degree; whether virgin maids or widows;

that shall after the passing of this Act, impose upon and betray into matrimony any of His Majesty's male subjects, by scents, paints, cosmetics, washes, artificial teeth, false hair, Spanish wool, iron stays, hoops, high-heeled shoes, or bolstered hips, shall incur the penalty of the laws now in force against witchcraft, sorcery, and such like misdemeanors, and that the marriage, upon conviction, shall stand null and void."

The mysteries of female toilette obviously worried the male lawmakers, but the desire to retain youthful good looks and beauty is as old as humankind. Many of the potions used sound utterly revolting: medieval women were urged to dab bats' blood onto their faces for an improved complexion, while American ladies in the 18th century used the warm urine of young boys to erase their freckles.

In 1845, the city of Boston, Massachusetts, passed a law that made it illegal to own a bathtub without a doctor's prescription.

banned LUXURIES

In Japan, income was what governed codes of social behavior during the Middle Ages. A peasant farmer was forbidden to build a house more than 36 feet long, and could only use bamboo thatch or straw for the roof, rather than wood. Inside, the floors were to be bare without floor mats. He was banned from serving fish or roast food at his daughter's wedding, his wife could only use hair combs made from bone and wood, rather than ivory or tortoise shell, and the men were not to wear stockings. This Spartan, and probably cold, existence served to keep the peasantry in their place in the social hierarchy for centuries.

Many laws, certainly in England, remain on the statute books long after they have become anachronistic. A law of 1336 prohibited anyone from eating more than two courses at any one meal, and another stated that anyone found breaking a boiled egg at the pointy end should have 24 hours in the village stocks. In Scotland, it is illegal to be drunk while in possession of a cow, and until recently in Chester, it was only legal to shoot a Welsh person with a bow and arrow outside the city walls after midnight.

In 1541 Henry VIII's Unlawful Games Act banned the playing of all sport on Christmas Day. The one exception to this was archery, which was permitted on the grounds of national defense. The point of the Unlawful Games Act was to ban certain sports which had diverted men from their archery practice, thus putting fletchers and bow-makers out of business and forcing them to travel abroad to make their living, "to the comfort of strangers and the detriment of the realm."

Outraged by the death of two guests who were poisoned by the Bishop of Rochester's cook, Henry VIII was determined to punish the perpetrator appropriately and ordered that he be boiled alive in his own pot. Unfortunately, the punishment for murder was hanging, but undeterred, the king changed the law so that the unfortunate cook could be boiled alive. Like many Renaissance princes, Henry was terrified of being poisoned, and the 1532 Act of Poisons can be seen as his personal insurance policy against such an eventuality.

Lending a hand

Mutilation in one form or another was an ancient method of punishment for a variety of crimes. In 1543, anyone who cast a blow that drew blood within royal precincts would have his right hand cut off; the final part of the Act details exactly which officials would perform the deed and who was responsible for cauterizing the stump and tending the wound afterward. Having cut off the offender's hand, the king was keen to revive him with a piece of bread and had the Sergeant of the Cellar on stand-by to administer "a pot of red wine...after his hand is so stricken and the stump seared." After all this ceremony, the one-handed offender was imprisoned for life.

history bites

sea queen

One of Ireland's most famous pirates was Grace O'Malley. Born in about 1530, her male relatives were noblemen and sailors, who acted as traders, ferrymen, and sometimes pirates. Violent conflicts between rival clans was a fact of life in 16th-century Ireland and Grace proved herself to be an effective leader of men—far better than her first husband, for example. She gathered 200 men under her control and used them to patrol the coast, either charging ships for protection or simply raiding them. She apparently gave birth to a son while at sea and the next day rose from her bed to see off the Algerian pirates who had the temerity to attack her ship.

Twice widowed and twice imprisoned, Grace spent a great deal of her life struggling against the English who were trying to impose their rule on Connaught. She was condemned for her piracy, although she seems to have earned the admiration of Sir Henry Sidney in Galway, who described her as "a most famous feminine sea captain ... a notorious woman in all the coasts of Ireland." In 1593 Grace traveled to London to plead with Elizabeth I to release her son and brother from prison, conversing with the Queen in Latin (which was possibly their only common language). A formidable woman, she achieved her aims, but what is probably more remarkable given her life of adventure and condemnation by the English as "a woman that hath impudently passed the part of womanhood and been a great spoiler and chief commander and director of thieves and murderers at sea," is that she died peacefully in her bed in 1603.

Lewd Theater

Given that the Elizabethan period is also remembered as the age of Shakespeare, it seems ironic that the government spent a great deal of time shutting down theaters and generally worrying that the outburst of dramatic creativity would corrupt the public. In 1593 the vice-chancellors of Oxford and Cambridge received a letter reminding them of their duties as "nurseries to bring up the youth in the knowledge and fear of God and in all manner of good learning," and demanding that they ban "common players" from the university precincts. The government deplored the fact that the students might be corrupted by plays that were "full of lewd examples and most of vanity," and conveniently forgot that some of these plays might actually have been written by some of the more talented students or graduates of the universities.

Bah Humbug

In 1677 an act of parliament ensured that Christmas Day was a day of rest for everyone—or nearly everyone. It stated that "no servant, artificer, workman, labourer or other person whatsoever shall do or exercise any worldly labours, business or worke of their ordinary callings" on Christmas Day. The key words were "ordinary callings" which implied that people could work as long as it was not in their normal job.

In 1646, the Roundheads' Long Parliament turned its attention to the excesses of the festive season and banned all Christmas dinners of more than three courses. Mince pies and Christmas pudding were also pushed off the menu, being described as "abominable and idolatrous."

gunpowder treason

In 1647, in another outburst of Puritan frenzy, the English Parliament banned all feasts and celebrations. The one remaining observance that was permitted was the commemoration of the Gunpowder Plot of 1605. Following the discovery of the Catholic plot to blow up the King in Parliament, the English celebrated every year with bonfires and sermons on 5 November. It is ironic that although Parliament was to sanction the murder of the king in 1649, the Gunpowder Plot remained as a celebration, although the Puritans did not intend to give thanks for the safety of the King, merely to remind everyone of the destruction of Papist ambitions.

SMOKE DEVIL

Of all the innovations and strange new items to emerge from the New World, tobacco has been one of the most contentious. From the outset, people were unsure of how to approach this strange new comestible and when a member of Columbus's crew was seen smoking on arrival back in Spain, he was arrested. People thought that the smoke emerging from his nose was a sign that he had been possessed by the devil.

FINAL SMOKE

James I of England penned a pamphlet in 1614 to express his intense dislike of tobacco, *A Counterblast Against Tobacco,* and in 1634 Tsar Michael of Russia forbade anyone to smoke or use tobacco on pain of death. The law was subsequently relaxed and by the end of the century, Russians caught smoking were punished far more leniently. They had their nostrils slit.

When Sir Walter Raleigh faced the scaffold for the second and final time in 1618, he arrived for his execution smoking a pipe, which apparently eased his nerves.

history bites

Civil society

When William Penn was granted a charter of settlement in North America by Charles II, he was reminded that he had permission to "reduce the savage natives by gentle and just manners to the love of civil society and Christian religion." No one bothered to ask the savage natives what they wanted, however.

Play the game

The laws of New England reflected many of those in Britain and simply attempted to maintain a godly, hardworking civilization. In 17th-century society, children were expected to earn their keep from a young age and were certainly not permitted the hours of leisure (or even education) afforded to children today. At the same time, the Pilgrim Fathers wanted to ensure that New England's youngest citizens grew up pure in mind and body. Laws specified that children were not to live near licensed premises such as taverns, nor were they permitted to play "corrupting games" such as cards and dice. Gaming was frowned upon for adults, too, but one particular law recommended punishment of the children caught with the dice, rather than the wicked people who taught them. "Children that play at cards or dice for the first offense be corrected at the discretion of their parents or masters, and for the second offense to be publicly whipped."

drawing the line

Punishment for sexual misconduct in 17th-century America was strict, with fines or imprisonment for adulterers and fornicators, and worse for convicted rapists. However, one cannot help feeling a little sorry for the joker Ralph Earle, who was fined 20 shillings in October 1663 for "drawing his wife in an uncivil manner on the snow."

stand and deliver

Highway robbery in England increased during the 17th and 18th centuries for two main reasons. The first was the introduction of a postal system and the second was because of the invention of the flintlock pistol in 1630. For the first time, soldiers, or in this case, thieves, were able to control a horse with one hand while aiming a lightweight pistol with the other. In 1782, Horace Walpole complained about the dangers of venturing out at night: ". . . one dare not stir out after dinner but well-armed. If one goes abroad to dinner, you would think one was going to the relief of Gibraltar."

history bites

In 1726 a Swiss visitor to England, César de Saussure wrote to reassure his family that the highwaymen were unfailingly polite and would do no harm as long as one surrendered all one's valuables. Both he and Walpole could perhaps take comfort in the knowledge that "All highwayman that are caught are hanged without mercy."

Seeking a Fortune

It is ironic that Dick Turpin (1703–1739), a reasonably successful highwayman, was arrested for killing a chicken. Turpin was a petty criminal who began his career robbing shops and housebreaking in rural Essex in the early years of the 18th century. In the 1730s, he took up the more lucrative trade of highwayman, robbing stagecoaches on the road or indulging in horse theft. Many of his legendary activities on his horse, Black Bess, are probably apocryphal, but after a brush with the law in London, Turpin fled to York where he adopted his mother's maiden name of Palmer and kept up a brisk trade in stolen horseflesh. When he was reported for shooting his landlord's hen, the authorities discovered his alias and his long list of felonies, and Turpin's career ended on the York gallows in 1739.

CRIME AND PUNISHMENT

a sea dog's life

Naval discipline was notoriously harsh and was rooted in medieval punishments. Richard I was the first English king to lay down a code of naval discipline and successive generations did little to alter it. In 1422, the *Black Book of the Admiralty* recommended that convicted robbers should have "boiling pitch poured over his head and a shower of feathers be shaken over to mark him, and he shall be cast ashore at the first land at which the Fleet shall touch." A man convicted of drawing a knife would lose a hand, and murderers were to be "tied to the corpse and thrown into the sea." Flogging was the most common penalty in the 18th and 19th centuries, and to add insult to injury, convicted offenders had 24 hours in which to make their own cat o'nine tails while locked in leg irons. The Army Act of 1881 finally abolished flogging in the British forces, as many believed it "made a bad man worse and broke a good man's heart."

Unofficial punishments were rife in the navies of the 17th and 18th centuries. Blasphemers were gagged and their tongues scraped, and persistent offenders could expect to have their tongues bored with a red-hot iron.

history bites

PROFITABLE SINS

The genial French Emperor Napoleon III (1808–1873) was once asked to abolish smoking, as many people regarded it as a terrible vice. Like many politicians since, Napoleon realized that he really could not afford to ban smoking. "This vice," he replied, "brings in a hundred million francs in taxes every year. I will certainly forbid it at once—as soon as you can name a virtue that brings in as much revenue."

A REAL PEARL

The last convicted stage coach robber in the USA was Pearl Hart, a woman of French-Canadian descent. An attractive woman born in about 1870, Pearl had separated from her husband and had joined up with a prospector named Joe Boot in Globe, Arizona, where they scratched out a meager living. In 1899, Pearl heard that her mother was dying back home in Toronto. Distraught and with no money to travel to her mother's bedside, Pearl and Joe hatched a plan to rob a stagecoach. They stripped the travelers of all their money and possessions, although Pearl relented and returned to give each of the three men a dollar apiece—"enough to eat on." The arrest of a female bandit caused a sensation and after three years in various jails, Pearl was pardoned before the end of her sentence, ostensibly because the prison "lacked accommodation for women prisoners." This was obviously a bit of a problem, but the governor was struggling to hide the truth: Pearl was pregnant. Apparently only two men had visited her—the prison chaplain and the governor himself.

on the throne

The electric chair was invented in the United States in 1882, and by 1889 it was used for the execution of criminals in New York. Impressed by what he heard about the machines, Emperor Menelik II of Abyssinia ordered three for his country in 1890. He was struggling to westernize the country and Menelik had signed treaties to build railways—but electricity had yet to be installed in the ancient kingdom. A disappointed emperor returned two of the chairs and kept a third for use as his throne.

Wicked Left-handers

Left-handed people have experienced all manner of strange legal prejudices over the centuries. In the Middle Ages, the Catholic Church declared that left-handers were servants of the devil; African tribes along the Niger river do not allow women to prepare food with the left hand because they fear the influence of sorcery. For generations in Japan, left-handedness in a wife was sufficient

history bites

grounds for divorce, because it was believed that the Japanese script could only be written successfully with the right hand.

tax evader

The American gangster Al Capone (1899–1947) was notorious for his racketeering in Chicago during the prohibition era. He was well known to the authorities for many years, but there was never sufficient evidence to convict him of a crime until 1931. Instead of prosecuting him on gangland charges, the Federal Tax authorities accused Capone of tax evasion and demanded millions of dollars in unpaid tax. Despite protesting that, "They can't collect legal taxes from illegal money," Capone was sentenced to 10 years in jail. Al Capone's business card stated that he was a used furniture dealer. It had a grain of truth as he was a keen collector of antiques and possessed a Louis XV writing desk among other treasures.

bird poop island

Under United States law, any American citizen may take possession of a foreign, uninhabited island on behalf of the USA as long as it contains bird droppings. When this law was passed in the 19th century, bird droppings (or guano) were a valuable source of fertilizer for farmland. Many islands were annexed under this law, including Christmas Island and Midway Island in the Pacific Ocean.

weed ban

Many drugs that are now illegal were freely available during the 19th century and early years of the 20th century. Marijuana was not outlawed in the United States until 1937, when Congress passed the Marijuana Tax Act. Even then, Congress did not ban the weed, but merely made it illegal to sell it without a license. No licenses were ever issued. Marijuana was completely banned in 1970.

gun slinger

One of the aphorisms of the Wild West was "God didn't make all men equal, Sam Colt did." Colt's new revolver—a handgun with a revolving chamber which allowed quicker firing—revolutionized gun design and was eventually adopted by the U. S. Army. Samuel Colt (1814–1862) patented the design in 1835, but his new gun design was not an instant success and the company he had established went bankrupt. At about the same time, his brother John was arrested and charged with killing a man, using, not one of his brother's guns, but an ax. Colt was outraged by his brother's choice of weapon and, never one to miss an opportunity for publicity, somehow persuaded the judge to allow him to demonstrate the superiority of his gun by staging a shooting display in the courthouse. Despite this diversion, John Colt was sentenced to hang for the murder.

debt negotiation

The outlaw Jesse James (1847–1882) was born in Missouri, the son of a Baptist minister. His career of robbery, violence, and murder somehow acquired mythological status even during his short lifetime, partly because journalists embroidered and romanticized his activities. He is believed to be the first man to carry out a successful daylight bank raid, relieving a bank in Liberty, Missouri, of $60,000 in 1872, and in 1873 carried out the first successful train robbery in the American West. He lived a peripatetic life as he and his gang tried to keep one step ahead of the law. Sheltering at a lonely farmhouse one day, the gang took pity on the widowed owner and gave her the money to pay off her considerable debts. The debt collector rode up and the widow paid him the $1,400 she owed. As he left, Jesse and the gang were lying in wait and robbed him, retrieving the money they had so "generously" given to their hostess.

Crime and Punishment

Turning Vegetarian

The murderer Alfred Packer (1842–1907) is widely known as the only man to be imprisoned for cannibalism in the United States. In fact, he was convicted for murder as cannibalism is not actually against the law. Packer was a gold prospector who set out with a group of 21 companions to explore the Colorado wilderness of Breckinridge in January 1873. They became lost and snowbound in the Rocky Mountains and Packer later confessed to roasting five of his colleagues, but insisted he only actually killed one of them and that was in self-defense. It was widely rumored that Packer became a vegetarian before his death in jail.

Maintaining Standards

The power exerted by gangsters, even from inside maximum security penitentiaries, often astonishes their lawyers. The legendary mobster Frank Costello (1891–1973), upon whom Marlon Brando modeled his performance in *The Godfather*, established a highly efficient crime syndicate in New York in the first half of the 20th century and his payroll included many policemen, politicians, and even military personnel. In 1951, after 30 years at the top of his profession, Frank was jailed. His standard of living inside jail was unbelievable and amazed his attorney Edward Bennett Williams. At 5 pm one day,

history bites

Williams told Frank he had been unable to get tickets for a performance of *My Fair Lady*. "Mr. Williams," said Costello, "You shoulda told me. Maybe I coulda helped." Williams admitted that he had not considered a jailed felon as a source for Broadway tickets, but when he arrived back at his hotel, he was astonished to find four tickets for that evening's performance waiting in his room.

mafia founder

"Lucky" Luciano (1896–1962), the man credited with founding the modern mafia in America, began his criminal life as a drug dealer, but had a keen eye for business and headed the National Crime Syndicate, an organization that took a percentage of many underworld deals. In 1936 Luciano was convicted on the testimony of prostitutes, many of whom had been bribed, and was sentenced to 30 years imprisonment. His influence did not decline, however, and in World War II, the government consulted with him about the whereabouts of German saboteurs in New York. Prior to the Allied invasion of Sicily and Italy, Luciano was also an unlikely military advisor, finding useful contacts in Italy to help American troops. His cooperation earned him a pardon in 1946, when he was deported to his homeland.

POLITICIANS

CReam OFF the top

Sir Robert Walpole (1676–1745) is regarded as Britain's first prime minister, although the office he held was officially titled First Lord of the Treasury. Political office was often a lucrative source of income in the 18th century and Walpole remained in office for 21 years, from 1721–1742. Although Walpole's political intentions were to avoid expensive foreign wars and to consolidate the Protestant succession of the Hanoverian monarchs, he also ensured that he and he alone controlled crown patronage. Walpole yielded immense influence and benefited from what was a perfectly legal practice: all government money flowed through his personal bank account and he was able to invest great sums and cream off the interest. This practice ended with Walpole, but by the end of his period of office he was seriously rich. He was a keen collector of art and his collection, which was sold to Catherine the Great by his grandson, formed the basis of Russia's magnificent Hermitage collection. By contrast, when William Pitt the Elder left office in 1761, he was so impoverished that he was forced to let his servants go and sell his horses.

history bites

Today, the peccadilloes of politicians are generally fair game for censure by political commentators and the newspapers, but society held different views 250 years ago. The only British prime minister to divorce his wife was the 18th-century Duke of Grafton. Although their marriage ended on the grounds of her adultery, the duke rather publicly kept a mistress, one Nancy Parsons, a well-known courtesan who lived above a perfumery shop in Soho.

irreplaceable greatness

Despite his own great achievements, Thomas Jefferson was a modest man and like many of his contemporaries, remained in awe of the illustrious Benjamin Franklin who was his predecessor as American ambassador to France in the 1780s. When Jefferson arrived in Paris, the French minister for foreign affairs welcomed him saying, "You replace Monsieur Franklin?" "No," Jefferson corrected him. "I succeed him. No one can replace him."

born and bred

But for an accident of fate, Napoleon Bonaparte would have been born an English citizen. His father, Carlo Bonaparte, was a Corsican nationalist who fought the Genoese for Corsican independence. In 1768, the Genoese accepted defeat, but instead of surrendering the island to the Corsicans, they sold it to the French. The Corsican rebels struggled against French domination, but were forced to surrender. Some of the leaders chose to go into exile and Pasquale Paoli, the leader, tried to persuade his friend Carlo Bonaparte to accompany him to England. Carlo was sorely tempted, but decided to stay simply because his wife was pregnant and the journey would be difficult for her. Later that year in 1769, their second son was born and named Napoleon.

Italian was the native language of Corsica and Napoleon did not learn French until he was 10 years old. Throughout his life his spelling remained dreadful, as did his pronunciation of many French words.

BLUBBERING FOOL

Viscount Goderich (1782–1859), an obscure, early 19th-century politician actually resigned from the job of prime minister before parliament convened—the only prime minister to do this. An emotional man, he was only in office for a few months in 1827, but was nicknamed "the Duke of Fuss and Bubble" because of his habit of bursting into tears. When King George IV appointed him, Goderich broke down in tears, and the king, possibly regretting his decision, called him a blubbering fool; when some of his ministers declined to serve, the tears flowed again, and during his final interview with the king, George IV had to lend Goderich his handkerchief to dry his eyes.

Goderich was succeeded by the far more manly Duke of Wellington, who was summoned to Windsor by the king early one morning. George IV was still in bed wearing his turban nightcap when he interviewed Wellington, giving him the job by saying bluntly, "Arthur, the Cabinet is defunct."

Pistols at dawn

The Duke of Wellington was the last serving prime minister to be involved in a duel. In 1829 he took exception to the Earl of Winchilsea's assertion that he was secretly a supporter of Catholic Emancipation [the proposal to allow Catholics full rights under English law]. Wellington had staunchly opposed this law, but by 1829 political expediency meant that he had to change his position. When Lord Winchilsea refused to apologise, however, Wellington demanded "the satisfaction for [his] conduct which a gentleman has a right to require and which a gentleman never refuses to give." In great secrecy, Wellington's doctor was asked to bring a case of pistols to Battersea Fields on 21 March 1829, where his second paced out the field to indicate where the participants should stand. "Damn it!" shouted Wellington, "Don't stick him up so near the ditch. If I hit him he will tumble in." Strangely for one of Britain's greatest military heroes, Wellington was an appalling shot, and was unlikely to hit his opponent. In the event, he shot wide and Winchilsea discharged his pistol into the air, muttered a suitable apology, and all parties were able to retire uninjured.

OLD PEELER

Sir Robert Peel (1788–1850) was an exceptional politician, whose lasting memorial to Britain was the formation of the police force. He was not a man of great charm, however, and Queen Victoria noted in her diary that he was "such a cold, odd man." His dedication to duty and refusal to court popularity probably saved his life, however, as in the days before photography, his face was not widely recognised by the populace. When an assassin tried to kill him, Peel's secretary became the victim, as the gunman failed to distinguish his real target.

the President's temp

America's least-known president is David Rice Atchison who served as the 12th president without even running for office. In 1849, James Polk left office and the incoming president Zachary Taylor refused on religious grounds to take the oath of office on a Sunday. The Constitution stipulated that the President Pro Tempore of the Senate should fill the position, so Atchison did so until Monday morning when Taylor was sworn in. Atchison's 24-hour term of office was quiet. He said, "I went to bed. There had been two or three busy nights finishing up the work of the Senate, and I slept most of that Sunday."

burning ambitions

In the years leading up to the Civil War, congressmen and senators debated the slavery question many times, and it was an issue that divided politicians on geographical as much as party lines. Democrat Stephen A. Douglas, one of Lincoln's rivals in Illinois, was anti-slavery and advocated a compromise in the new state of Kansas, whereby the people could vote on the issue of whether or not to adopt it. His views made him extremely unpopular in some quarters, however, and he remarked that, "I could travel from Boston to Chicago by the light of my own effigies."

mass appeal

Napoleon III of France (1808–1873) came to power—and held on to it—by playing shamelessly to the poorer classes and gagging the press. He declared the rights of men to choose their masters, endowed public works that benefited the poorer sections of society, and regulated the price of bread, which was subject to appalling fluctuations. He was a man of considerable vision, and one of the little-known legacies of his reign is margarine. He asked a chemist to develop a food product for the bread of "the army, navy, and needy classes of the population." The result was margarine—a cheap and long-lasting substitute for butter.

Laying it on with a trowel

Benjamin Disraeli (1804–1881), prime minister of Britain twice in the 19th century, was a great favorite of Queen Victoria, who rewarded him with the title Earl of Beaconsfield for his hard work. Disraeli not only secured the title of Empress of India for the Queen, but he knew exactly how to ingratiate himself in his audiences with her, remarking to the writer Matthew Arnold that, "Everyone likes flattery and when you come to Royalty, you should lay it on with a trowel."

His political rival, William Gladstone, somehow lacked the social skills necessary to impress the Queen and in 1878 she noted in her diary, "One other great quality which Lord Beaconsfield possesses—which Mr. Gladstone lacks entirely—and that is a great deal of chivalry and a large, great view of his Sovereign's and country's position."

When Disraeli died in 1881, the Queen was bereft, but she didn't know that Disraeli had declined a deathbed visit from her, saying

history bites

"No it is better not. She would only ask me to take a message to Albert."

cowboy president

America's vice-president is only a heartbeat away from power, but every vice-president who has suddenly been catapulted into the presidential hot seat must find the experience both exhilarating and terrifying. Of course, political power bases also shift with the rise of a new man to power, and allies of the previous president are not always keen on the newly elevated political star. When President McKinley was assassinated in 1901, his campaign manager, Mark Hanna, was appalled by the prospect of Theodore Roosevelt in the White House. "I told William McKinley it was a mistake to nominate that wild man at Philadelphia," said Hanna on McKinley's funeral train. "Now look, that damned cowboy is President of the United States!"

cough up

Stanley Baldwin (1867–1947) was President of the Board of Trade in the years immediately after World War I, when Britain had run up enormous debts. Baldwin was increasingly worried by the size of the debt and wrote an anonymous letter to *The Times* urging the wealthier part of society to pay a voluntary tax in an effort to relieve the burden. Baldwin calculated that if the rich paid out a sum equivalent to about a sixth of their estate, the national debt would be alleviated. Baldwin himself invested £150,000 ($285,000)—about 20 percent of his fortune—in government bonds and then destroyed the certificates, so he had effectively made a gift to the Treasury. Not surprisingly, Baldwin was something of a lone voice for this cause and the rest of the upper classes were slow to follow his example.

shot down

Eloquent and inventive politicians are often good at damning their opponents in the most skillful terms and Winston Churchill was one of the best. Churchill's career was colorful—he swapped parties twice and enjoyed a long rivalry with his fellow prime minister Stanley Baldwin. Baldwin was the antithesis of Churchill in many ways, being cautious and lacking the flamboyance of the younger man. Churchill delighted in baiting him, and once said, "I wish Baldwin no ill, but it would have been much better if he had never lived."

mickey mouse leader

Adolf Hitler (1889–1945) was responsible for unleashing untold devastation and misery on the world, but despite this he was apparently kind to small children and fond of animals. It is apparent from this entry in the diaries of Joseph Goebbels the Nazi propaganda minister, that Hitler enjoyed watching Walt Disney's *Mickey Mouse* cartoons. Goebbels presented him with 18 movies in 1937, noting without irony that the Führer seemed "very happy" with his Christmas gift. "I hope that this treasure will bring him much joy and relaxation," he added.

Poisoned debate

Nancy Astor (1879–1964) was the first female MP to take her seat in the British House of Commons in 1919 and although she was a formidable woman, even she found the experience of being the only woman among over 600 men a little unnerving. However, she soon found her feet and espoused the causes of women's rights and temperance. One implacable opponent was Winston Churchill; although they moved in the same social and political circles, the two politicians detested each other. They especially disagreed over women's emancipation and during one heated exchange, Nancy exclaimed, "Honestly Winston, if I were married to you, I would put poison in your coffee." "And if I were your husband," Winston shot back, "I'd drink it."

Politicians

Nancy Astor traveled to Russia in 1931 to see the effect of Stalin's Communist reforms. Stalin was interested to hear her opinions of Winston Churchill, at that time politically discredited. "Finished!" she said with some delight, and told Stalin that he could write him off. "I don't agree," replied Stalin with a flash of foresight. "You will send for the old war-horse yet, in the day of battle."

Military Leaders

Throughout history, many successful generals have gone on to carve out a second career as high-ranking politicians, or even as presidents or prime ministers. Wellington, Grant, and more recently Colin Powell are just three examples. Not all military men are so keen to remain in the political limelight, however. In 1884, General Sherman was asked to accept the Republican nomination as presidential candidate. Sherman replied in the trenchant manner for which he was famous. "If nominated, I will not accept. If elected, I will not serve."

After World War, II more than one general had his eye on the White House. Both MacArthur and Eisenhower considered the job, and Ike took some time before deciding which party to support. When they discussed the matter soon after the war's end, Eisenhower fervently believed that military men should not become president. He was completely sincere in his belief, but MacArthur cast him a sideways glance, saying, "That's the way to play it, Ike." Eisenhower was elected president in 1952.

chip off the old block

Jan Smuts (1870–1950), South African prime minister during World War II, was not a man renowned for subtlety or finesse of expression, yet his position obviously meant that he was required to mingle with the great and good from around the world. In 1947, he was invited to London to attend the wedding of Princess Elizabeth and Prince Philip. A man of few words and not naturally given to small talk, he found himself next to the bride's redoubtable grandmother, Queen Mary. "You are the big potato," he said. "All the other queens are small potatoes," a comment that was somehow flattering to the queen, but possibly not to the other assembled queens, most of whom were her relatives.

what's your inscription?

During the 1950s, the foreign secretaries of Britain, France, and the Soviet Union met at a summit meeting. Relaxing over a drink, Bevin pulled out his gold watch to check the time. It was inscribed with a dedication: "To Ernest Bevin, in memory of forty years of devoted service to the Dockers' Union." Georges Bidault showed his companions his watch, which was inscribed "*Pour Georges de la part de ses parents, a l'occasion de sa majorité.*" They turned to Khrushchev and asked to see his watch, so he reluctantly showed them. It was a beautiful antique Cartier watch which was inscribed "To His Imperial Highness, the Grand Duke Constantine, from his fellow members at the Hurlingham Club, 1913."

nothing to hide

Winston Churchill (1874–1965) was not only a highly successful prime minister and politician, he was also a great character, and there are many stories about his wit and eccentricities. Famous for sustaining himself with whisky and sodas and champagne, he noted, "I have taken more out of alcohol than alcohol has taken out of me." He used to dictate letters to his secretaries from his bath and once emerged to find President Roosevelt waiting for him in his bedroom. Undeterred, Winston said, "The Prime Minister had nothing to hide from the President of the United States."

hair to stay?

At first glance the physical characteristics of the Russian leadership of the 20th century could not be more different, from the patrician last tsar, Nicholas II, to the thick-set peasant features of Leonid

Brezhnev. An intriguing pattern has emerged, however. Bald men have alternated with more hirsute politicians in an unbroken line from Nicholas II to Vladimir Putin, so much so that a future election may be influenced, with voters favoring not the best leader, but the man with the finest head of hair.

Failed attempts

Frederick Forsyth's novel *The Day of the Jackal* deals with a fictional plot to assassinate the president of France in the 1960s, but there were several real attempts on the life of President de Gaulle. A tall man with a distinctive profile, he was easily recognized in a crowd and De Gaulle was especially at risk when Algeria was struggling for independence from France. In August 1962, his motorcade was attacked on the outskirts of Paris as anti-independence terrorists fired on his car, puncturing the tires and shattering the rear window. Fortunately the president was unhurt, and as he got out of the car he remarked, "They really are bad shots."

Sleeping with the president

Republican Thomas Dewey ran for president of the United States twice, in 1940 and again in 1948. When he campaigned against Truman in 1948, he was widely expected to win. The Democrats, had, after all, been in power since 1933 and the economic fortunes of the country were poor. Harry S. Truman was not an especially charismatic candidate and even his wife Bess expected him to lose. Dewey was governor of New York, and it seemed that all he needed to do to beat Truman was look good and speak in platitudes. By election day, all of the polls predicted a Republican victory and as Dewey retired for the night, he said to his wife, "How will it be to sleep with the President of the United States?" "A high honor", she replied, "and quite frankly darling, I'm looking forward to it." However, Truman's immense campaigning efforts paid off, and contrary to all the predictions he was re-elected for a second term. At breakfast the next morning Mrs. Dewy turned to her husband and said, "Tell me Tom, am I going to Washington, or is Harry coming here?"

thinking voters

Adlai Stevenson (1900–1965) was highly respected as an exceptional American statesman. He campaigned twice for the presidency, in 1952 and 1956, but was beaten both times by Eisenhower and in 1960 lost out on the Democratic nomination to John F. Kennedy. Some of his most valuable work was at the San Francisco Conference that founded the United Nations in 1945. He was known to be a cerebral campaigner and was rightly admired for this, but he knew it was not enough to win. After one speech, one supporter gushed, "Every thinking person will be voting for you, Senator." But Stevenson wryly replied, "Madam, that is not enough. I need a majority."

Stevenson was an accomplished public speaker and delighted in telling a story about another admirer who praised his speech. He replied that he was thinking of publishing it posthumously. "Oh won't that be nice" came the reply. "The sooner the better."

Legless dictator

In 1838, after he lost his leg in battle against the French, the Mexican dictator General Antonio Santa Anna gave it a solemn funeral at Santa Paula churchyard. As Santa Anna was president-dictator with a reputation for shooting enemies of the state first and asking questions later, the turnout for this service was reassuringly high.

WRiTERS and aRTiSTS

baLD PaTCH

Legend has it that the ancient Greek playwright Aeschylus was killed by a falling tortoise. This unlikely accident occurred when an eagle, which had seized a tortoise, was looking for somewhere to smash its shell and spotted the bald pate of the playwright. Aeschylus was killed as the falling tortoise landed precisely on target.

honoRed dead FLy

The Romans have become almost a byword for excessive living, with tales of orgies and extravagant parties abounding in the literature of the period. The writer Virgil (70–19 BC), best known for his epic poem *The Aeneid,* made his own contribution to the myths by hosting a lavish funeral for a dead housefly. No expense was spared—the mourners (many professionals, paid for by the poet) joined celebrities at Virgil's mansion on the Esquiline Hill in Rome to hear eulogies and poems composed in the fly's honor. The fly was finally buried in a large mausoleum at an estimated cost of $100,000 in today's money.

Virgil was not motivated entirely by frivolity, however. He had heard that the government planned to confiscate the property of the rich and redistribute it to war veterans, but properties that contained burial grounds were to be exempt. The law was shortly passed and Virgil succeeded in preserving his property.

criminal knight

One of the first books printed by William Caxton, what he called a tale of "the noble acts, feats of arms of chivalry, prowess, hardiness, humanity, love, courtesy, and very gentleness," was actually written in prison by a knight accused of rape, violent assault, and theft. The author of *The Morte D'Arthur* was probably Sir Thomas Malory, an English knight of the shires and one-time Member of Parliament. He lived during the Wars of the Roses, a period of civil war in England when rival claimants fought for the throne, and it is likely that some of Malory's alleged crimes were politically motivated smears by his enemies. Having lived a blameless life, it appears that Malory suddenly went off the rails in 1450, when he was accused of three extortions, two rapes, and cattle rustling. Imprisoned for several years, Malory devoted himself to consolidating, translating and adding to the Arthurian legends, producing a lyrical tale of courtly love that owed little to his apparently criminal background.

OLD CROW

The great 17th-century intellectual Thomas Hobbes (1588–1679) was much admired by contemporaries for his wisdom and the breadth of his learning. He was born prematurely, apparently because his mother went into labor when she heard that the Spanish Armada was approaching. His greatest work, the *Leviathan* was published in 1651 and encompassed metaphysics, psychology, and political philosophy; it set out to explain how mankind is driven by enlightened self-interest and in depicting the world in this materialist light, Hobbes managed to offend his royal patrons and the Church.

By the end of his long life, however, he was well respected, and John Aubrey wrote in his memoir, "I have heard his brother Edmund and Mr. Wayte his schoolfellow say that when he was a Boy he was playsome enough, but withall he had even then a contemplative Melancholinesse. He would get him into a corner, and learne his Lesson by heart presently. His hair was black, and his schoolfellows were wont to call him Crowe."

TRUE PORTRAIT

The most famous portrait of Oliver Cromwell (1599–1658) shows an uncompromising man gazing out at the world with a thoughtful expression. It is not a handsome face and the ravages of time and disease are clearly visible, which was unusual in portraits of potentates. The artist, Peter Lely, earned his reputation as an accomplished painter with his portraits of Charles I's courtiers, most of whom presumably preferred flattering visions of themselves. The ascetic Cromwell was rather different and instructed the artist, "Mr. Lely, I desire you would use all your skill to paint my picture truly like me, and not flatter me at all; but remark all these roughnesses, pimples, warts, and everything as you see me, otherwise I will never pay a farthing for it."

enemy cause

John Milton (1608–1674) was an enthusiastic supporter of the Parliamentary cause during the English Civil War, and abandoned his poetry to write several polemical pamphlets during the 1640s. The author of a spirited defense of the regicide, Milton was an official under Cromwell, but later in life he knew he had made a number of enemies and according to one contemporary "he was in Perpetual Terror of being Assassinated; though he had Escap'd the Talons of the Law, he knew he had Made Himself Enemies in Abundance. He was So Dejected he would lie Awake whole Nights." After the Restoration of the monarchy in 1660, Milton was offered a job as Latin Secretary, the same post in which he had served Cromwell. Much to his wife's chagrin, Milton declined the job on ideological grounds. "Thou art in the right," he said. "You, as other women, would ride in your coach; for me, my aim is to live and die an honest man."

dress rehearsal

The fourth Earl of Chesterfield (1694–1773) is best remembered for his letters to his son, which were daily epistles of guidance in the ways of good manners and worldly behavior. In part, they are models of world-weariness and cynical advice, obviously reflecting the noble earl's character. At the end of his life, he became weakened by disease and his daily carriage rides proceeded at a snail's pace. An acquaintance stopped to congratulate him on making the effort to get out. "I do not come out so much for the air," replied Chesterfield, "as for the benefit of rehearsing my funeral."

Little Pope

Alexander Pope (1688–1744) is rightly revered as a giant of English literature, but was a little less imposing in the flesh. Crippled by a tubercular infection of the spine when he was a child, he failed to grow properly and was only 4 ft, 6 inches high as an adult. Rather unkindly, he was described as a "crazy little carcass of a man," and had to resort to wearing clothes of stiff canvas to support his spine and keep his body erect. He disguised the withered appearance of his legs by wearing several pairs of stockings.

His physical problems partly explain his early devotion to literature, but they did not prevent him mixing with society. In 1714 he was delighted to be invited to the home of the Earl of Halifax (a poet himself) to read selections of his recent translations of Homer's *Iliad*. Sadly, the noble lord was not terribly enthusiastic and noted a few sections that he felt needed more work. Pope retired rather crestfallen. On the advice of his friend and fellow poet Samuel Garth, Pope did not call on Halifax again for several months. When they next met, Pope expressed gratitude for the Earl's suggestions and read him some of the corrected sections. Halifax was impressed and congratulated Pope, but with the passage of time, had not spotted that Pope had made no alterations at all to his work.

tyrant's symphony

Ludwig van Beethoven (1770–1827) was a great admirer of Napoleon and the ideals of the French Revolution. In 1803, after a trip to Paris, he intended to dedicate a symphony to him, a powerful work he called the "Bonaparte Symphony." However, when he heard that Napoleon had crowned himself emperor in defiance of all republican ideas, Beethoven furiously erased his hero's name from the work with such force that he broke his pen. He complained to his assistant Ferdinand Ries that Napoleon had now become a tyrant and that he would not dedicate any music to such a man. The symphony was re-named the "Eroica Symphony" and had its premier in Vienna in 1805.

independent thought

The Romantic poets were renowned for their non-conformity and desire to shock their readers and society. Percy Bysshe Shelley (1792–1822) was known as "Mad Shelley" even when he was at school at Eton. He exhibited a total disregard for social convention by leaving his wife and two children to elope with 16-year-old Mary Wollstonecraft. He was a radical and an atheist at a time when such attitudes were highly provocative. When the poet drowned in 1822, Mary was left to raise their son alone, and a friend advised her to send him to a school where he would be taught to think for himself. "To think for himself!" his mother exclaimed, perhaps remembering the consequences of her husband's independence of mind, "Oh my God, teach him to think like other people!"

old bones

The source of the tongue twister "she sells sea shells on the sea-shore" is thought to lie with the early 19th-century fossil hunter Mary

Anning. In 1812, Mary, a poorly educated Dorset girl, uncovered and then pieced together the fossilized remains of a prehistoric marine animal, the ichthyosaurus. An unlikely paleontologist, Anning made her living from selling fossils and stones she found under the crumbling cliffs of Lyme Regis, Dorset.

Comic Romance

Jane Austen's novels were extremely popular in the author's lifetime (1775–1817), and the Prince Regent himself kept a set of her works in each of his residences. In 1816, after the publication of *Emma*, the Prince's secretary wrote to Miss Austen, suggesting that she might like to pen "an historical romance, illustrative of the history of the august house of Coburg." To her eternal credit, Jane Austen did not allow her head to be swayed by royal condescension and interest and wrote back very firmly, "I could no more write a romance than an epic poem. I could not sit seriously down to write a serious romance under any other motive than to save my life; and if it were indispensable for me to keep it up and never relax into laughing at myself or other people, I am sure I should be hung before I had finished the first chapter."

WRITERS AND ARTISTS

high art

Eloquent, learned, and unworldly, Samuel Taylor Coleridge
(1772–1834) was one of the great Romantic poets. He was a close
friend of Wordsworth and from 1797 they inspired each other,
debating poetry and the intellectual and political problems of the age.
It was Wordsworth who encouraged Coleridge to write *The Rime of
the Ancient Mariner,* and in his turn, Wordsworth's *Poem to
Coleridge,* eventually became *The Prelude.*

Their literary activity was aided and abetted by opium and this
may have accounted for the fact that Coleridge's legendary loquacity
was sometimes unintelligible, even to his closest friends. One
biographer reported that he held forth for over two hours, "during
which Wordsworth listened to him with profound attention, every now
and then nodding his head as if in assent."

At the end, the poet Samuel Rogers admitted that he simply did
not know what Coleridge had been talking about, and asked
Wordsworth whether he had understood Coleridge's lecture. "Not
one syllable of it," he responded.

heady presence

The philosopher and advocate of utilitarianism, Jeremy Bentham
(1748–1832), argued that the objective of all legislation should be to

achieve "the greatest happiness of the greatest number." He developed what he called a "hedonic calculator," which gauged the effect of various actions on the populace and was highly respected by his peers.

He helped to found University College, London, to which institution he bequeathed his body, where it still resides to this day. Bentham's will stated that his body should be preserved as an "Auto Icon" dressed in one of his suits and "seated in a chair usually occupied by me when living."

When Bentham died, his request was carried out, although his head was poorly embalmed and has since been replaced by a wax replica. It regularly goes missing, often stolen by undergraduates for a bet. University College regularly records their founder's presence at College Council meetings with the words, "Jeremy Bentham—present but not voting."

widely traveled

Sir Humphrey Davy (1778–1829) has achieved lasting fame as a great scientist, who advanced the knowledge of chemistry in the 18th and early 19th centuries. Like so many people in the Enlightenment, however, his interests ranged widely into cultural spheres. In his youth Davy assisted with the publication of Wordsworth's *Lyrical Ballads* and was a friend of the writer Sir Walter

Scott. He traveled widely throughout Europe, but it is clear that he had few pretensions as an art lover. When a friend asked him what he thought of the great art galleries in Paris, he replied, "The greatest collection of frames I ever saw."

FOLLOWING SUIT

William Wordsworth (1770–1850) was appointed poet laureate in 1843, although some of his contemporaries in the literary world seemed to think that the former radical poet had "sold out" to the Establishment. In his poem *The Lost Leader*, Robert Browning wrote disparagingly, "Just for a handful of silver he left us,/Just for a riband to stick in his coat."

During his seven years as laureate, Wordsworth wrote nothing. When he attended the formal ceremony of appointment, he had to borrow a suit from a friend as he did not possess anything smart enough. In 1850, when Tennyson succeeded him, he borrowed the same suit of clothes.

TOILET HUMOR

Alfred, Lord Tennyson (1809–1892) was revered as one of the great poets of the Victorian era, his work popular with a great tranche of the population from Queen Victoria downward. He was known among his friends for his eccentricities, however, and he delighted in amusing house guests at his home on the Isle of Wight with his impressions of people going to the lavatory.

Tennyson remained reasonably fit into old age, and once proudly told the actress Fanny Kemble, "I can run uphill, I can waltz." The young Miss Kemble crushingly replied, "I hope I shall never see you do it."

Food for thought

Tennyson's sister Emily was also regarded as eccentric. She was fond of animals and in old age always dined with her raven and lapdog. She divided all her food into three portions, the first for the lapdog, the second for herself, and the third for the raven, which was attached to her wrist by a short lead.

Writer's block

Many writers have become frustrated with the demands of their publishers and, believing that they could do a better job, have established a publishing company. Sir Walter Scott (1771–1832), the author of many immensely popular historical novels, was one of the most successful writers of his era and went in to business with Constable and Company. The company pioneered the advance system, whereby an author was paid for his work before it was actually written, and Scott took full advantage of it. By 1825 he had contracted to write nine books and had received advances of £10,000 ($19,000). Unfortunately, the company went bankrupt in 1825 and rather than being rich, Scott owed the enormous sum of £121,000 ($230,000). The only way to pay off the debt was to write his way out of it, and Scott worked terrifically hard for four years before the strain precipitated a stroke. Scott had managed to pay off a third of the debt by the time of his death and the rest was settled by the sale of his copyrights in 1847.

best sellers

Wilkie Collins (1824–1889) delighted in his friendship with the greatest English writer of the 19th century, Charles Dickens. Twelve years his junior, Collins undoubtedly looked up to Dickens and in 1854 dedicated his third novel, *Hide and Seek* to Dickens "as a token of admiration and affection." Dickens returned the compliment and was obviously impressed with Collins work. The two men were very close and in 1860 Collins' brother married Dickens' daughter Kate. Toward the end of Dickens' life, however, relations between the two writers soured. Dickens died in 1870 and only three years later John Forster's *Life of Charles Dickens* became a best-selling biography. After Wilkie Collins' death in 1889, his library was sold and some of his true feelings about Dickens' work can be seen from the marginal notes in his copy of Forster's biography. Forster began his biography with the words, "Charles Dickens, the most popular novelist of the century." To which Collins added "after Walter Scott."

Vicious Rumor

The 19th-century writer Harriet Beecher Stowe was the author of the most famous piece of anti-slavery literature to emerge from the USA. *Uncle Tom's Cabin* was written in 1852 and caused a sensation, catapulting its author to celebrity. In addition to writing more than two dozen books, Stowe also penned articles for popular magazines and may be the source for scurrilous rumors about Lord Byron. In 1869, she met Byron's widow and went on to write an extraordinary article, "The True Story of Lord Byron's Wife," in which she accused Byron of committing incest with his sister Augusta.

Family shame

It is often the case that writers and artists are not fully appreciated by their own families or friends. The accomplished journalist and contemporary of Dickens, William Thackeray (1811–1863) was also a highly acclaimed writer and the author of *Vanity Fair*, but one night when he was kissing his young daughter goodnight, she turned to him and said, "Papa, why do you not write books like *Nicholas Nickleby*?"

woman scorned

When Wilkie Collins published what has remained his most famous novel, *The Woman in White* in 1860, he received many letters of admiration and congratulation, praising his skilful plotting and brilliant characterizations. There was one dissonant voice, however. "Excuse me if I say, you do not really know a villain. Your Count Fosco is a very poor one, and when you next want a character of that description I trust you will not disdain to come to me. I know a villain and have one in my eye at this moment that would far eclipse anything that I have read of in books. Don't think that I am drawing on my imagination. The man is alive and constantly under my gaze. In fact he is my own husband."

These words would have been stunning enough from a stranger, but in fact they came from Rosina Bulwer-Lytton, the estranged wife of Collins' acquaintance the writer Edward Bulwer-Lytton.

poems from beyond the grave

When Dante Gabriel Rossetti's beautiful wife Elizabeth died in 1862, Rossetti was grief-stricken and he buried her with the manuscript of the poems he was working on, many of which had been inspired by her. Seven years later, Rossetti realized that the only copy of a number of his verses resided with his wife's corpse, and there was only one way to retrieve them. Accordingly, Mrs. Rossetti was disinterred and the poems, once dusted off and wiped down with disinfectant, were just about legible. Rossetti's friends, who had performed this grisly and rather selfish task, told the poet that Lizzie had looked remarkably well. When the poems were finally published in 1870 they were well reviewed by the critic Robert Buchanon in an essay entitled, "The Fleshly School of Poetry."

Knocking aspiring authors

Benjamin Disraeli (1804–1881) enjoyed a reasonably successful career as a writer before he embarked on politics, but his literary reputation ensured that aspiring authors often sent him their manuscripts. Disraeli formulated a characteristically cunning reply: "Thank you for you manuscript. I shall lose no time in reading it."

George Bernard Shaw (1856–1950) replied in a similarly withering manner to a young author who had sent him a long and rather tedious manuscript. "The covers of your novel," he wrote back, "are too far apart."

The illustrious 18th-century writer Samuel Johnson (1709–1784) was also in great demand as an arbiter of literary skills. One aspiring writer was delighted when the great man told him that his manuscript was both good and original. "Alas," Johnson continued, "What is good is not original and what is original is not good."

Joining the Silence

Sir Lewis Oxford (1833–1907) was a minor Victorian poet who wrote in a similar style to Tennyson. He obviously felt that his outpourings, such as *Songs of Two Worlds*, and *The Epic of Hades,* which consists of monologues by various characters from Greek mythology, were worthy of more critical respect. He complained to Oscar Wilde that he had not even been considered for the post of poet laureate. "It is a complete conspiracy of silence against me—a conspiracy of silence!" he cried. "What ought I to do, Oscar?" "Join it," Wilde replied.

Not That Bad, but Not Good Either

The 19th-century poet, writer, and educational reformer Matthew Arnold (1822–1888) was revered and feared in equal measure for his critical intellect and occasionally difficult behavior. While staying in America he was offered some pancakes by his hostess and he passed the plate to his wife, saying, "Do try one, my dear. They're not nearly as nasty as they look."

history bites

Lina Waterfield recalled in her autobiography that the great poet arrived at her house when she was a child of six. She was unable to read and Arnold expressed his displeasure: "It is disgraceful, and you must promise me to learn at once; if you don't I shall have to put your father and mother in prison." Tall, with impressive whiskers, Arnold was a forbidding figure to a small child and Lina was terrified by the threat. She sought reassurance from her father, who only partially comforted her by saying he thought it unlikely that Arnold could exercise judicial powers, "although he is a Government Inspector of Schools."

When Arnold died in 1888, Robert Louis Stevenson remarked, "Poor Matt. He's gone to Heaven, no doubt, but he won't like God."

saucy family secrets

The explorer Sir Richard Burton (1821–1890) was also a gifted linguist and published lyrical translations of the *Arabian Nights* and the *Kama Sutra*, as well as numerous accounts of his travels, many with intriguing titles, such as "Notes on Scalping." He had to resort to privately publishing the *Kama Sutra* and *The Perfumed Garden,* in order to avoid prosecution: the subject matter was just a little too erotic for Victorian sensibilities. Many of his works did not survive him as his wife burnt many of his papers on his death, possibly to preserve her husband's reputation as a gallant explorer and to hide his more prurient interests from his legions of admirers.

dying art of writing

Mark Twain was born in November 1835, shortly after the appearance of Halley's Comet, which returns to Earth every 76 years. Twain often fancifully linked himself to the comet and commented that having arrived together, they would depart together. Incredibly, he was proved right. He died in April 1910, and on the night of his death the comet could be seen blazing a trail across the night sky.

Twain was a trailblazer himself in many ways, and was probably the first writer to submit a manuscript to his publisher that was not handwritten. Twain was an early adopter of the typewriter and used a Remington to type out *The Adventures of Tom Sawyer*.

Despite the lasting appeal of Tom Sawyer and Huck Finn, Twain spent the last two decades of his life in financially straitened circumstances and supplemented his income with lecture tours across Europe and America. He was mightily amused when a reporter tracked him down in London on a commission to discover whether the great man had died. "If Mark Twain has died in poverty send 1,000 words," read the cable from the editor of the *New York*

Journal. Twain was keen to help the young reporter, and famously cabled back "Reports of my death greatly exaggerated."

unappreciated talent

In his later years, Rudyard Kipling (1865–1936) acquired a reputation as the "poet of the British Empire," for his novels and short stories set in India. His talents were not always appreciated however. In 1889, when he had already published *The Man Who Would Be King,* the editor of the *San Francisco Examiner* declined to publish an article he had written. "I'm sorry Mr Kipling, but you just don't know how to use the English language," he wrote in his letter of rejection.

In 1907 Kipling was awarded the Nobel Prize for literature, "in consideration of the power of observation, originality of imagination, virility of ideas, and remarkable talent for narration."

struggling writer

D. H. Lawrence (1885–1930) struggled against the strictures of his humble background to become a writer. The son of a miner, Lawrence won a scholarship to Nottingham Grammar School and with the help and encouragement of his mother earned a degree at Nottingham University. He was devoted to his mother and was distraught when she died of cancer in 1910. However, he was pleased that she lived just long enough to see and hold his first published novel, *The White Peacock*.

However, his father was not an educated man and struggled to read the first page, preferring instead to discover how much his son had earned for the book. When Lawrence told him he had been paid £50—a considerable sum at the time—his father was flabbergasted. "Fifty pounds! An' tha's niver done a day's hard work in thy life!"

NEVER GROW UP

Famous as the author of *Peter Pan*, Sir James Barrie (1860–1937) also wrote a number of plays for the stage, notably *The Admirable Crichton.* On one occasion he received a telegram from an ambitious understudy telling him that the show's star had been taken ill and that he would be tackling the leading role. Barrie did not attend the performance, but sent back a reply, which read, "Thanks for the warning."

TALL ORDER

George Bernard Shaw (1856–1950) was a towering figure in the world of English literature for the first half of the 20th century. He was a tireless and prolific writer, devoting himself not only to plays, but also to politics. An early socialist, he also supported women's suffrage and the abolition of private property.

He was in constant demand as a speaker and at social functions. At one party, the hostess saw him standing alone and asked anxiously, "Are you enjoying yourself, Mr. Shaw?" "Certainly," he replied, "there is nothing else here to enjoy."

Bernard Shaw was married for 45 years, although he continued to enjoy the company of young, beautiful, witty women. He was once approached by the famous American dancer Isadora Duncan, who playfully suggested that they should have a child together. "Think of it," she enthused, "With my body and your brains, what a wonder it would be!" "Yes", replied Shaw dolefully, "But what if it had my body and your brains?"

neglected writer

G. K. Chesterton (1874–1936) was an ebullient man and a writer of great wit and energy. A journalist, poet, critic, and novelist, he remains one of the great neglected writers of the 20th century. His output was prolific and he was often in demand as a speaker. When asked which book he would most like to take to a desert island, Chesterton replied, "*Thomas's Guide to Practical Shipbuilding*."

Organization was not one of his strong points, however, and he remarked that he did much of his writing at railway stations, as he invariably missed his train. He once cabled his wife, saying, "Am at Market Harborough. Where ought I to be?"

SURE TO BE READ

Chesterton was great friends with the writer and poet Hilaire Belloc (1870–1953). The two men shared a common outlook on politics and religion to the extent that George Bernard Shaw nicknamed them "Chesterbelloc." Perhaps influenced by Belloc, Chesterton converted to Catholicism in 1922, but Belloc failed to attend the service. In 1936 when his friend died, Belloc not only attended the requiem mass, but also managed to sell the obituary of his friend to no less than four newspaper editors.

Writers usually want to be remembered by posterity, but no one put it more succinctly than Belloc:

"When I am dead, I hope it may be said:

'His sins were scarlet, but his books were read.' "

BURNING WILDE

The legendary actress Sarah Bernhardt (1844–1923) was as famous for her temperament as for her extraordinary dramatic skills. By the

1880s she was famous throughout Europe for her emotive talent and for the seductive charms that few men could resist. The great actress did not see eye to eye with Oscar Wilde, however, and they quarreled over the interpretation of her role in *Salomé*. Wilde retired and asked, "Do you mind if I smoke, Madame?" To which Bernhardt retorted, "I don't care if you burn."

In 1915, Bernhardt injured her leg so badly that it had to be amputated, but she carried on acting, often in plays where roles were written especially for her. While she was recovering from the accident, the manager of the Pan American Exhibition in San Francisco sent an unusual telegram asking to exhibit her leg, and offering $100,000. Bernhardt sent a pithy reply: "Which leg?"

not this war

During World War I, any young man of military age who was not wearing uniform in public was viewed with suspicion as a possible "conchie" (conscientious objector). When the writer Lytton Strachey (1880–1932) was confronted by a woman demanding why he was not "fighting for civilization," he replied, "Madam, I am the civilization for which they are fighting." Strachey was also forced to appear before a tribunal to answer for his beliefs. "I understand, Mr. Strachey," began the chairman, "that you have a conscientious objection to all war." "Oh no, not at all," replied Strachey. "Only to this war."

PROFITABLE HOBBY

T. S. Eliot (1888–1965) is widely regarded as the most influential poet of the 20th century. American-born, after he graduated from Harvard, he studied in Germany and eventually settled in England. In 1915 his first acclaimed piece, *The Love Song of J. Alfred Prufrock* was published in *Poetry* magazine and was followed in 1922 by the challenging masterpiece *The Waste Land*. Despite his talent, life as a poet did not pay the bills and from 1917 until 1920, Eliot worked in Lloyds Bank, where he proved diligent and exacting in his work. Indeed, one of his superiors, believed that "our young Mr Eliot's" hobby probably helped him in his bank work, remarking, "I don't see why—in time, of course, in time—he mightn't even become a branch manager." Eliot, although gratified by the ambitions of his boss, left Lloyds in 1925 to work at the publisher's Faber and Faber. He went on to win the Nobel Prize for literature in 1948.

FORMIDABLE TRIO

Edith, Osbert, and Sacheverell Sitwell were a formidable literary trio in the first half of the 20th century, famed for their erudition, wit, and aesthetic pronouncements, as well as for their writing. Their parents, Sir George and Lady Ida were eccentric and often distant parents. Osbert hated his schooldays, noting that, "Public schools are to private schools as lunatic asylums are to mental homes: larger and less comfortable." Sir George was something of a polymath and invented a number of unusual items, such as a revolver for shooting wasps and a rectangular egg composed of meat, for use by sportsmen.

Fiery Fruit

John Steinbeck (1902–1968) took the title of his best-known work, *The Grapes of Wrath*, from the lyrics of the *Battle Hymn of the Republic*—"Mine eyes have seen the glory of the coming of the lord. He is trampling out the vintage where the Grapes of Wrath are stored." It was a powerful title for an epic novel about the trials of living in the dust bowl of America during the Depression years, and the novel sold well worldwide. It was translated into many languages, including Japanese, where the title became "The Angry Raisins."

bloomsbury hothouse

Outstanding literary and artistic talent, as well as rivalries, jealousies, and love affairs characterized the hothouse literary world of the

WRITERS and ARTISTS

Bloomsbury group in the early years of the 20th century. Writers and artists such as Virginia Woolf, Vanessa Bell, E. M. Forster, and Lytton Strachey discussed and encouraged each other's work. Leonard Woolf, the husband of Virginia, ran the Hogarth Press that published many titles, including, in 1927, Virginia Woolf's *To the Lighthouse*. Virginia sent a proof copy to her close friend the writer Vita Sackville West, inscribed "Vita from Virginia. (In my opinion the best novel I have ever written.)" The immodest inscription puzzled Vita as Virginia was usually rather self-effacing. It was only when she turned the next page that she discovered the joke: the book was a dummy copy, and all the interior pages were blank.

too many dwarfs

Two of the finest British writers of the 20th century, J. R. R. Tolkein and C. S. Lewis were great friends and met every week or so in an Oxford pub. They discussed their work from time to time, and bounced ideas off each other. When Tolkein announced yet another addition to the already long list of characters in *The Lord of The Rings*, Lewis replied in mock despair, "Not another wretched dwarf!"

history bites

undesirables

Prior to Operation Sealion, the planned German invasion of England in 1940, the Nazis drew up a list of "undesirable" citizens, people who would have been imprisoned or worse under the Third Reich. In 1945, the list was discovered and was found to contain many writers and artists, including the novelist Dame Rebecca West and the actor Noel Coward. West immediately sent Coward a telegram: "My dear—the people we should have been seen dead with!"

misguided fame

Most writers enjoy basking in the admiration of their readers. In his autobiography, the great comic writer P. G. Wodehouse recalled sitting next to a lady who told him that her sons were great fans of his work and purchased every novel as soon as it was published. Wodehouse, was duly gratified, until she concluded, "And when I tell them that I have actually been sitting at dinner with Edgar Wallace, I don't know what they will say."

no kisses please

The attentions of literary fans are often harder to bear in the flesh than in letters. James Joyce was once approached by a devoted fan in Zurich, who asked to kiss "the hand that wrote *Ulysses*." Joyce refused and replied, "No, it did lots of other things too."

STAR STRUCK

The redoubtable Dr. Samuel Johnson reveled in his literary reputation in 18th century London and rarely hesitated to oblige his audiences with a string of witty remarks. He was once surrounded by a group of young ladies who felt overwhelmed to be in the company of such greatness to the extent that that they could do little more than look and point at him. Johnson regarded them with amusement, before saying, "Ladies, I am tame; you may stroke me."

UNSTOPPABLE HEMMINGWAY

F. Scott Fitzgerald (1896–1940) and Ernest Hemingway (1899–1961) enjoyed and endured a literary rivalry. Fitzgerald did not particularly like Hemingway but realized, not without envy, that he was a superbly talented author. "He's a great writer," Fitzgerald admitted. "If I didn't think so, I wouldn't have tried to kill him. I was the champ and when I read his stuff I knew he had something. So I dropped a heavy glass skylight on his head at a drinking party. But you can't kill the guy. He's not human."

history bites

Fitzgerald was joking, but Hemingway was blessed with an extraordinarily strong constitution. In 1954, he experienced two plane crashes within 48 hours in Africa and somehow survived injuries that would have killed a lesser mortal: a ruptured liver, kidney, and spleen, crushed vertebrae, concussion, and temporary loss of hearing and eyesight. In addition, he suffered myriad hunting and sporting accidents, and punished his body with a lifetime's heavy drinking, only to commit suicide by shooting himself in 1961.

PROLIFIC ARTIST

The artist Pablo Picasso (1881–1973) spent much of World War II in Paris, which was occupied from 1940 by the Germans. He found himself the subject of unwanted attention from the Gestapo, and was visited by two officers who noticed Picasso's famous picture *Guernica* that depicted the destruction of Barcelona by German planes during the Spanish Civil War. "Did you do that'" asked one of the Germans. "No," replied the artist. "You did."

According to the *Guinness Book of World Records,* Picasso was the world's most prolific artist, with a credited 13,500 paintings, 100,000 prints or engravings, 34,000 book illustrations, and 200 sculptures or ceramics to his name.

WRITERS and ARTISTS

biting wit

The mordant wit and biting ripostes of Dorothy Parker (1893–1967) disguised an unhappy private life and a lifelong battle with depression. After an affair with a married reporter, an unwanted pregnancy, and a subsequent abortion, Parker drank heavily and attempted suicide twice. Her friends could do little to stop her, but Robert Benchley tried to warn her in perhaps the only way she would appreciate. "Dottie," he said, "if you don't stop this sort of thing, you'll make yourself sick."

time limited novels

Georges Simenon (1903–1989) was a prolific novelist, most famous for his series of detective novels about Inspector Maigret. Like many popular novelists, Simenon considered his Maigret novels inferior to his more serious, but less bankable, works of literature. He devoted exactly 11 days to each of these literary pieces, devoting his whole time to the book in hand. He began by having a thorough medical examination, then he cancelled all appointments, and refused to answer the phone. He sketched out a rough plan on the back of an envelope and then "became" the main character in the novel. Simenon's "serious" works are considerably shorter than the Maigret novels, simply because the author could not sustain his peculiar regime for any longer than 11 days. "It's physical, he said. "I am too tired."

over his head

In a similar vein, the novelist Douglas Adams, author of *The Hitch-Hiker's Guide to the Galaxy* had to be locked in a hotel room by his publishers in order to finish his work. Adams famously could not stick to even the most extended deadlines, remarking, "I love deadlines. I especially like the whooshing sound they make as they go flying by."

disasters and disappointments

Precious bulbs

One of the strangest speculative ventures in history revolved around tulip bulbs in 17th-century Amsterdam. Until 1593 what is now the national flower of Holland had never been seen in Europe; tulips were originally wild flowers and were grown in Turkey. The novelty and scarcity of the flowers when they were first imported into western Europe ensured that they would be reassuringly expensive and many people began to deal in bulbs, speculating upon the huge demand for tulips. At the height of "Tulipmania," one bulb could buy an entire landed estate, but when the bottom fell out of the market, you were lucky to swap a bulb for a common onion.

Swapping cards

Faced with a chronic shortage of coins in Canada in 1685, and unable to pay the army, the governor requisitioned all the playing cards in the colony and used them as official currency. He ordered that the cards could be accepted for payment of anything within the colony. With the arrival of the next ship from France, the cards were recalled and cashed in for metal currency. But the problem did not end there and after 1690 the substitution of paper or cards for coins of the realm became an annual occurrence, leading to an incredible 400 percent inflation in 1713. People became so confused by the use of bills of exchange and other IOUs that in 1729 they actually petitioned the King to reintroduce the playing card system.

dubious shares

The South Sea Company was established in 1694 to exploit the trade with Spanish colonies in South America, and in 1711 it was granted a monopoly over this trade in return for a $13 million loan to the government to pay off the national debt. When war with Spain erupted again in 1718, there was little prospect of any money being made from trade, but shares continued to change hands on the basis of future prosperity that would undoubtedly emerge after the war. By 1720, shares had risen terrifically and many extraordinary schemes were launched on the back of the South Sea Company's success to relieve speculators of their money, the most ludicrous being "A company for carrying-on an undertaking of great advantage but no-one to know what it is." Incredibly, even this obviously bogus company amassed $3,000 of investment. As one pamphleteer wrote, "I heard of Men of low Degree, being advanced to their Coaches."

disasters and disappointments

In February 1720 shares were $325; by June the price was $1,750, and from then on the air began to leak out of the bubble. By the end of September, shares were $300 and a great many fortunes had been lost. The King, George I had prudently sold his before the bubble burst, as had the poet Alexander Pope, but many others were not so lucky. Riots broke out, Parliament was recalled, and a committee was formed to investigate the South Sea Company; naturally many of the most important men had disappeared abroad.

expanding tastes

The infamous French predilection for eating horsemeat is a relatively recent taste, and was borne out of the extreme adversity of the siege of Paris in 1870, when the population of the city came near to starvation. Hemmed in by Prussian forces, the Parisians refused to surrender the city, but two months into the siege food prices had risen by a third and traditional supplies of meat had run out. The Parisian diet diversified and expanded, and top of the new menus was horsemeat, closely followed by cat, dog, and rat. The population of the city zoo declined, as the popular elephants Castor and Pollux were sacrificed for the good of the people. Lions and tigers were spared, simply because they were too difficult to catch (although in a city full of soldiers, it can't really have been all that difficult). It is estimated that the citizens consumed 65,000 horses, 1,200 cats, 500 dogs, and 300 rats. Nobody touched the apes and monkeys: recent Darwinian theories about the evolution of the species meant that eating them was regarded as tantamount to cannibalism.

LOSS OF FACE

The competition between the "Great Powers" in the later years of the 19th century would have been laughable, had it not been conducted with the most powerful weaponry in the world. Germany and Britain vied to have the largest empires and, in particular, state-of-the-art navies.

In 1889, seven warships from three navies were anchored in the tiny Samoan harbor of Apia, which was really not big enough to accommodate them, but national pride demanded that the warships remain, despite the impending dangers. It was typhoon season, the barometer was sinking, which signalled a storm at the very least. The ships were so closely packed together in the small port that the rough seas of a tempest would undoubtedly smash the ships against each other.

Despite the strong meteorological signs, none of the ships' captains would leave the harbor for fear of losing face. When the typhoon struck, four ships sank, another was flung onto the beach and only a British cruiser escaped destruction by sailing headfirst into the storm. Two hundred lives were lost to maintain national pride in a small colonial outpost.

the great prediction

It is always hard to predict the vagaries of the Stock Market, but few people predicted the great Crash of 1929. One highly respected economist, Irving Fisher opined two weeks before the crash, "In a few months I expect to see the stock market much higher then today ... a severe depression such as 1920–1921 is outside the range of probability." The crash of 1929 heralded a terrible decade of economic depression for the USA and Europe, and Fisher himself lost the equivalent of $140 million.

where's the nearest gas station?

In the world of engineering, precise measurements and accurate calculations are absolutely critical. Mechanics responsible for fueling a new Air Canada Boeing 767 were not only confused by the mass of fuel needed, but compounded the problem by getting the conversion from imperial to metric units wrong as well.

Scheduled to fly from Montreal to Edmonton, the plane took off without enough fuel in the tanks, and some distance short of the destination, first one, then the other engine stopped working: the plane had run out of gas. Fortunately, the pilot was able to glide to safety on a nearby abandoned air force runway, where the plane landed safely and was only slightly damaged by a small fire in the nose cone. This was put out by handheld extinguishers from the Winnipeg Sportscar Club who were enjoying a family day on the old runway.

Air Canada immediately sent a team of mechanics to investigate the problem. Their car ran out of gas on the way to the air base.

Flying boats

As early as 1920, far-sighted people realized that the most lucrative way forward for airpower was to begin passenger flights. The Italian Count Caproni designed an incredible airplane that began life as a houseboat. It was intended to carry 100 passengers across the Atlantic and required three sets of triple wings, along with eight engines. It was not the most aerodynamic of designs, but managed a 60-foot test flight before the nose dipped sharply and sent the aircraft crashing back into the water of Lake Maggiore.

it ain't over until bing sings

For the USA, the end of the Vietnam War was a depressing and humiliating episode after over a decade's fighting. The evacuation from Saigon at the end of the Vietnam War in April 1975 was a confused, chaotic period, with many people fighting for a place on the evacuation aircraft to escape the forces of Viet Minh. The evacuation operation "Frequent Wind" was implemented by the U.S. Marines and Air Force to evacuate U.S. staff and selected Vietnamese personnel.

Bizarrely, the signal given for all Americans to prepare for evacuation was a weather forecast stating that "The temperature is 105 and rising!" which was followed by the broadcast of Bing Crosby's "White Christmas" over the Armed Forces Radio Network.

hotline for a cold war

During the years of the Cold War from 1950 to 1989 the world hovered on the brink of a nuclear confrontation many times. The Americans have admitted at least 20 incidents that nearly led to disaster and the Russians probably experienced at least an equal number of near misses. A "hot line" linked Moscow and Washington from 1963, but the risk of misunderstanding remained, especially during periods of heightened tension.

In 1956 during the Suez crisis, NORAD believed that unidentified aircraft were airborne over Turkey. NATO jets were poised to intercept them, when the message came through from an eyewitness that the planes were actually a flock of swans. Six years later when the world teetered on the brink again during the Cuban Missile crisis, an intruder tripped a security alarm at Duluth, which in turn activated alarms at local bases. The alarm at Volk Field, Wisconsin misfired and triggered the signal for nuclear-armed jets to take off. Back at Duluth, personnel discovered that the intruder was a bear.

miLiGaRy mayhem

chasing his tail

The ancient Greeks used fast runners as couriers between the city states, and these men played an especially vital role in wartime. In 490 BC the Persians under Darius the Great, embarked with a 30,000-strong army across the plain of Marathon, 25 miles from Athens. The Athenians prepared to fight the invaders, knowing that the independence of Greece was at stake. They dispatched their fastest runner, Philippides, to alert the Spartans and enlist their help. Incredibly, he covered the 150-mile journey in two days, but he seems to have traveled in vain, because back in Marathon, the Greeks decided to launch a surprise attack upon the Persians without waiting for the Spartans. With a force of only 10,000 men, the Athenians beat back the Persians and sent a runner back to the city with the good news. He was evidently made of less stern stuff than Philippides, because he collapsed and died after his 25-mile journey, just managing to announce, "Rejoice, we conquer!"

The modern marathon owes its length to neither of these stories, but to the 1908 London Olympics. The marathon course started at

Windsor Castle and traveled 26 miles, 385 yards, to the royal box at White City Stadium.

threatening letter

Philip II of Macedon was one of the great leaders of ancient times, perhaps eclipsed only by his son Alexander the Great. Philip succeeded in uniting the major Greek city states of Athens and Thebes before turning his attention to the Spartans, the notoriously disciplined and isolationist people to the south. Instead of unleashing his forces, he sent the Spartans a threat to intimidate them. "You are advised to submit without further delay, for if I bring my army into your land, I will destroy your farms, slay your people, and raze your city." The Spartans were unmoved and sent back a chilling and uncompromising reply: "If."

getting knotted

Alexander the Great repeatedly demonstrated the quick thinking necessary for any successful military leader. At Gordium in 333 BC Alexander cheated the prophecy that foretold that rule over the East would only be achieved by someone who could undo the intricate Gordian knot. Frustrated by the bark knot, and obviously dismissive of the old prophecy, Alexander simply cut it in half with his sword.

Military Mayhem

Alexander was probably not the first and certainly not the last ruler to keep one eye on how posterity would judge him. When he was finally forced to retreat west after his stupendous eastern invasions, he ordered his men to build an abnormally large camp containing artifacts that were larger than life. He intended this to be his memorial, hoping he and his men would go down in history as superhuman soldiers. As the Roman historian Quintus Curtius Rufus noted, "His intention was to make everything appear greater than it was, for he was preparing to leave to posterity a fraudulent wonder."

mixed blessing

Pyhrrus, king of Epirus (*c.* 319–274 BC) was the most successful general of the ancient world after Alexander. He is best remembered for his struggles with Rome; in 280 he crossed the Aegean with 25,000 men and a number of elephants to support the Tarentines, a Greek colony in the south of Italy who were being oppressed by Rome. He is not remembered for the remarkable feat of transporting elephants to Italy, but for the long and bloody battle against the Romans on the River Siris. According to Plutarch, 15,000 men (on both sides) died in the battle and Pyrrhus ruefully remarked, "If we are victorious in one more battle with the Romans, we shall be utterly ruined." This, of course, was the first "Pyrrhic victory."

history bites

After a glorious military career Pyrrhus was killed in street fighting in Argos, when a Spartan woman threw a tile at him that knocked him out and enabled another Spartan to behead him.

one-sided Fight

In 320 BC, an army led by Ptolemy I of Egypt crushed the mighty citadel of Jerusalem which had withstood attacks by the finest fighting forces of the day, resisting Sennacherib and Nebuchadnezzar. Although the Egyptians probably attributed their victory to the strength and tenacity of their troops, the reason behind the victory is a little more prosaic. Ptolemy had cunningly attacked the city on the Sabbath, and the Jews were forbidden to fight on their holy day, even in self-defense.

brave WARRIOR meets Final end

Attila the Hun (c. 406–453) led the nomadic tribes that emerged from the steppes of central Asia to challenge the might of the Roman Empire. Fearless fighters and superb horseman, the Huns fascinated Roman observers, who could scarcely believe that a group "so little advanced in civilization" could be such deadly soldiers. Their success was attributed to their speed and ability to "pillage the camp of their enemy almost before he has become aware of their approach."

Attila became leader of the Huns in 434 and induced so much fear among his enemies that the Romans called him the "Scourge of God." Having devastated every country between the Black Sea and the Mediterranean, he led the Huns as far west as France, where they were finally defeated at the Battle of Chalons in 451. Undeterred, Attila invaded Italy the following year and wreaked havoc among many of the northern cities.

It is ironic that after a life of battle, Attila died in 453 in his own bed. He suffered a nose bleed on his wedding night and it is said that he was so inebriated after the wedding celebrations that he actually drowned in his own blood.

Viva el Cid

The Spanish medieval hero Rodrigo Díaz de Vivar, (*b.* 1043), better known as *El Cid* ("the fighter") succeeded in keeping a high profile even after his death. Realizing how vital a leader's presence in battle was for troops' morale, his dying wish was that his body should be embalmed and seated on his horse Babieca. El Cid was fatally wounded while fighting the Moors in 1099, but his body was preserved until the Spaniards' defense of Valencia, the city founded by El Cid himself. King Bucar of Morocco was on the point of defeating the Spanish, when El Cid miraculously appeared mounted on his horse at the head of his troops, who rallied at the sight of their hero and pushed back the Moors.

nothing personal

In 1199, Richard the Lionheart lay dying from an arrow wound that had infected his shoulder with gangrene. He knew that he did not have long to live and set his affairs in order. One of his last acts was to ask to see Bertram de Gourdon, the Frenchman who had shot him. "What harm did I ever do you that you should kill me?" the king asked rather plaintively. De Gourdon obviously saw no reason to lie or try to plead for his life and gave the king a straight answer: "You killed with your own hand my father and two of my brothers and you likewise designed to have me killed." Remarkably, his answer filled Richard with remorse and he ordered the prisoner to be given 100 marks and set free. Unfortunately, after Richard's death, his courtiers were not so forgiving: they captured De Gourdon and flayed him alive.

germ warfare

In 1349, the population of England and Wales was decimated by the Black Death, the plague that had spread virulently across the country.

Military Mayhem

The sheer numbers of people killed nearly caused a breakdown in society and in the northern city of Durham there were riots. People rightly feared that the Scots would take advantage of English misfortune to invade the country, and indeed they did exactly that in the summer. A great army gathered at Selkirk intending to invade the whole English realm, but in an act of unwitting germ warfare, they were quickly infected with the plague germs and 5,000 men died. The rest retreated home carrying their germs with them. Although the spread of the plague seems to have been slowed by the Scottish winter, it broke out again in the spring of 1350. John of Fordun, author of the *Scotichronicon* sadly recorded, "For this plague vented its spite so thoroughly that fully a third of the human race was killed. At God's command, moreover, the damage was done by an extraordinary and novel form of death. Those who fell sick of a kind of gross swelling of the flesh lasted for barely two days ... It generated such horror that children did not dare to visit their dying parents, not parents their children, but fled for fear of contagion as if from leprosy or a serpent!"

All or Nothing

Bertrand du Guesclin (1320-1380) was one of the most famous French soldiers of the Hundred Year War and an outstanding military hero. He fought at a time when the chivalric ideal was at its height, but his behavior sometimes fell short of the knightly ideal. After one battle, Guesclin had helped to defeat the English and took many of them prisoner. The prisoners should then have been shared out among the French knights, so that they could be ransomed, but Guesclin could not reach agreement with his colleagues. They agreed that the fairest solution was simply to kill all of them, even though this contravened the chivalric code and the unwritten rules of war. Accordingly, 500 English soldiers were massacred in cold blood outside the gates of Bressière.

blind ambition

One of the most remarkable and imaginative military leaders in 15th-century Europe was the Bohemian mercenary Jan Zizka (*c.* 1360–1424). Ziztka fought for the English at Agincourt, joined the Teutonic knights to attack the Poles, and finally joined the Hussites in Prague in 1419. Zizka's strength was in allowing his peasant armies to fight with roughly hewn but deadly weapons, rather than forcing them to conform to conventional fighting tactics. Lacking cavalry, he also improvised armored carts, which mounted small howitzer cannons and could be pulled through enemy troops, mowing them down in the same way as tanks. What was most remarkable was that Zizka was blind in one eye from childhood and lost his remaining eye at the siege of Raby in 1421. His best victories were achieved when he was totally blind.

alien invasion

Horses had been extinct in the Americas for about 10,000 years until reintroduced by Columbus. On his second voyage in 1493, he transported horses to Hispaniola and gradually in the early years of the 16th century they populated the North American continent as the Conquistadors imported them to speed their exploration of the New World. In 1519, when he had captured Mexico, Hernan Cortes notably said "Next to God, we owe our victory to our horses," and he did not exaggerate.

As well as being beasts of burden, horses were useful weapons of intimidation. The Aztecs had never seen anything like a man mounted on a horse and believed that they were witnessing the arrival of supernatural beings when they first encountered the Spanish in 1519. Cortes noted that they "thought horse and rider were all one animal," and although Cortes and his men had only 16 horses, the Aztecs were so frightened by them, they submitted to him at once.

history bites

Lend us your ear

Wars break out for all sorts of reasons, but rarely over small body parts. The War of Jenkins Ear is one of the more ridiculously named conflagrations in British history. It began when Britain exacted revenge on the Spanish for cutting off the ear of Captain Robert Jenkins, who duly preserved it and presented in to Parliament in 1739. War was declared in October 1739, much to the delight of the people, although the prime minister Sir Robert Walpole observed glumly, "They may ring their bells now, they will be wringing their hands before long."

Bitter revenge

Benedict Arnold is infamous as the American patriot who turned traitor and betrayed his countrymen to the British during the Revolutionary War, conspiring to sell them West Point, and then fighting against his former comrades. The reasons for his betrayal seem as complex as the man himself. In the early years of the war Arnold proved himself brave and ruthless, but he was also ambitious and felt that his achievements went unnoticed by his superiors. He was injured twice in the same leg, wounds that virtually crippled him. In 1778, he became commandant of Philadelphia, where he was seen to live beyond his means and Congress wanted to court martial him for misappropriating public funds. Arnold wrote bitterly to George Washington, "Having become a cripple in the service of my country, I little expected to meet [such] ungrateful returns." Financial ruin loomed and, his pride wounded, Arnold began to negotiate with the British, who promised him $18,000 and a commission for his services. His behavior outraged his countrymen and when Thomas Jefferson heard of Arnold's perfidy in selling West Point, he exclaimed, "If we catch him we'll cut off that American leg and bury it with honor... the rest of him we'll hang!"

brave men and women

War has generally been men's work, but until the mid-19th century many armies went into battle accompanied by camp followers, a trail of women, families, and other hangers-on who helped to support the main force. There are a number of tales of women who found themselves in the line of fire by accident. American children are often told the story of "Molly Pitcher," the woman who was made a sergeant by George Washington for her bravery. Molly Hays was at the battle of Monmouth Courthouse in June 1778, where her husband William was an artilleryman. Molly was bringing a pitcher of water to the hot and thirsty soldiers when her husband was injured. Molly instantly joined the depleted gun crew, helping to fire the weapon. She carried on undeterred even when an enemy cannon shot passed right between her legs, damaging only her petticoat. According to legend, she observed that it was lucky it did not pass a little higher, for in that case it might have carried away something else.

favorite horse

Napoleon Bonaparte's (1769–1821) first real military success came at the siege of Toulon in 1793 where French royalists had united with a British fleet to besiege the naval base. Revolutionary forces were under severe pressure and their performance was not helped by the fact that they were led by two incompetent generals, Jean Carteaux and Francois Doppet, one of whom was a former portrait painter, the other a dentist who fainted at the sight of blood.

Like many great generals, Napoleon had a favorite horse. The stallion Marengo had been captured in Egypt in 1798 and Napoleon rode him during most of his famous campaigns, including the second Italian campaign, the retreat from Moscow, and at Waterloo. As an artilleryman, Napoleon was not a natural horseman and his aides made sure that all his horses were perfectly trained before he rode them. His devoted valet wrote, "The Emperor mounted a horse without grace... and I believe that he would not have always been so sturdy on the horse if we had not taken so much care to give him only horses perfectly trained." Others were more brutal in their assessment of the emperor's equestrian skills: "Napoleon rode like a butcher," recalled one observer.

Napoleon had between 10 and 18 horses killed under him in battle, but Marengo was captured by the British at Waterloo and sent back to London to be exhibited in Pall Mall, where he was a sensation. His skeleton can still be seen today in the National Army Museum, Chelsea.

hate thy enemy

Horatio Nelson (1758–1805) is Britain's most famous naval hero, rightly revered as the victor of many great sea actions, the greatest being the defeat of the French at Trafalgar in 1805. The Royal Navy was (and is) an institution of strict hierarchy and Nelson's advice to a young midshipman is worth repeating. "Firstly you must always implicitly obey orders, without attempting to form any opinion of your own regarding their propriety. Secondly, you must consider every man your enemy who speaks ill of your king; and thirdly you must hate a Frenchman as you hate the devil."

The Duke of Wellington, the other great hero from this era, echoed Nelson's sentiments, writing proudly, "We always have been, we are, and I hope that we always shall be detested in France."

history bites

mind your head

No one ever joined the navy for a luxurious life and many sailors in the 18th and 19th centuries were press-ganged into service against their wills. The press gang may have filled ships, but it certainly did not produce keen, high-caliber recruits and the Admiralty cannot have been too surprised when they discovered in 1815 that one in every thousand men was a certified lunatic—this was seven times the national norm of one person in every 7,000.

Although alcoholism and venereal disease were partly blamed, the most common cause for naval madness was apparently because men repeatedly hit their heads on the low beams below decks, which caused brain damage.

harsh punishment

Military discipline was notoriously harsh and was enforced by flogging, so that soldiers and sailors feared their own commanders more than the enemy. British soldiers in the 18th century were known by the rather grim nickname of "Bloodybacks." By the time of the War of 1812 between Britain and the USA, it was clear that American sailors performed just as well, if not better than their British enemies, despite a less punishing regime on board ship. It is really not surprising that so many British sailors deserted to crew American ships and enjoy an improvement in their living conditions.

have one on me

It was usual for sailors who died at sea to be buried in the deep, but when Lord Nelson died at the moment of victory at Trafalgar, it was clear that England's greatest hero should receive a fitting funeral. Nelson's body was placed in a barrel of brandy to preserve it and shipped to Gibraltar, where the preservative was changed to spiced wine. The barrel was lashed to the mast of HMS *Victory* and guarded day and night. When *Victory* reached London, the admiral's body was transferred to a coffin and Nelson received the state funeral he deserved. A popular rumor circulated that thirsty sailors took a few sips from the brandy cask holding the admiral's corpse, which is why it had to be topped up at Gibraltar, and this gave rise to the naval phrase, "tapping the admiral," referring to illicit drinking.

Stiff Upper Lip

After Waterloo many of the wounded had to endure amputations in grim conditions in the days before anesthetics, but there were a great many brave men who withstood the pain with barely a whimper. Lord Fitzroy Somerset's shoulder had been smashed by a musket ball and he apparently suffered the amputation of his entire arm without a sound. The Prince of Orange, who was lying injured nearby was not even aware that an operation was taking place until Lord Fitzroy called out to an orderly, "Bring back my arm. There's a ring my wife gave me on the finger."

Possibly the most famous injury at Waterloo, and an incredible display of the British stiff upper lip, was the loss of Lord Uxbridge's leg. Uxbridge and Wellington were surveying the battle from their horses when a canon ball smashed into Uxbridge's right knee. Uxbridge looked down in some surprise and said "By God sir! I've lost my leg!" Wellington lowered his telescope and leant over to examine the injury. "By God, sir so you have!" he replied, and called calmly for stretcher-bearers.

shattering illusions

Wellington harbored few illusions about the men he led. Many of the enlisted soldiers and sailors had been forced to join the military, either by their own unfortunate circumstances, or by impressments. Although the military at least offered a hot meal and a uniform, the life was harsh and unrelenting. Wellington called his army "the scum of the earth," and knew that most men did not join out of patriotism for their country. "People talk of their enlisting from their fine military feeling—all stuff—no such thing. Some of our men enlist from having got bastard children—some for minor offences—many more for drink."

Enemy Sacrifice

Wellington's down-to-earth sentiments were echoed a century later by General George Patton, who had no time for romantic notions about sacrificing oneself for one's country or romantically dying in battle. "The object of war is not to die for your country," he said, "but to make the other son-of-a–bitch die for his!"

Napoleon He Ain't

Nineteenth-century Mexico was a shrinking state, despite the bombastic confidence of the man who was president at least four times. General Antonio Lopez de Santa Anna (1797–1876) liked to be known as the "Napoleon of the West," but in fact he was utterly unlike his hero. Physically, he was Bonaparte's opposite, being tall and slim, and after 1838, one-legged. (He lost his leg fighting the French at Vera Cruz.) Nor did he have Napoleon's military skill: in 1836 he lost Texas after an 18-minute battle in which a small Texas force wiped out a far more numerous Mexican army.

history bites

Leading from the back

One of the more unlikely commanders of the British army was Lord Raglan, who was appointed to lead British troops to the Crimea in 1854, despite the fact that he was 65 years old, had only one arm, and had never actually led troops on the field of battle. Raglan had been with Wellington at Waterloo (before he succeeded to his title he was known as Lord Fitzroy Somerset) and throughout the Crimean campaign kept referring to the French as the enemy, when they were actually the British allies.

The last ones to know

Many of the wars fought by the British Empire were carried out with only the most minimal interference from the government in London, simply because of the time it took to send a dispatch of orders. In November 1814, Britain and the USA concluded the War of 1812 with the Treaty of Ghent, but the news took over a month to filter through to the commanders in the field.

In December, English veterans under Sir Edward Packenham (the brother-in-law of the Duke of Wellington) continued to besiege New Orleans. In January 1815, he launched an ill-advised assault on the town, which was skillfully pushed back by American troops under General Andrew Jackson. British losses were severe (and included

Packenham), whereas American casualties were light, but all of them were unnecessary given the peace treaty that had been concluded a few weeks earlier.

Spilling Blood

The American Civil War was fought by commanders who had been colleagues and even friends in the years before 1861, and communications between opposing leaders were usually conducted with great courtesy. In 1864 Confederate troops under General J. B. Hood attacked Union positions in Tennessee, but where possible encouraged their enemies to surrender in order to "avoid an unnecessary effusion of blood." In 1864, Hood wrote to the commander of the garrison of Resaca, Georgia, demanding "the immediate and unconditional surrender" of the post. He received a confident reply from the commanding officer: "I have to state that I am somewhat surprised at the concluding paragraph to the effect that, if the place is carried by assault, no prisoners will be taken. In my opinion I can hold this post. If you want it, come and take it. I am general, very respectfully yours, your most obedient servant, Clark T. Weaver."

history bites

switching sides

Robert E. Lee (1807–1870) is probably the only general in history to have been offered command of the opposing armies in a war. Lee was a highly respected and experienced soldier and both the Union and Confederate governments wanted his services. He felt ripped in two by the problem, feeling that his duty as an officer lay with the elected government, but as a southerner he could not fight against the people and ideals he held dear. As his letters show, he intended to retire from the fray, but only two days after his resignation, the Confederate government at Richmond, Virginia asked him to lead the Rebel forces. Lee explained to his sister, "With all my devotion to the Union and the feeling of loyalty and duty of an American citizen, I have not been able to make up my mind to raise my hand against my relatives, my children, my home. I have therefore resigned my commission in the Army, and save in defense of my native State, with the sincere hope that my poor services may never be needed, I hope I may never be called on to draw my sword."

pride before a fall

"Fighting Joe" Hooker was regarded as one of the most skilled northern generals early in the Civil War, and he certainly didn't lack confidence. At the battle of Chancellorsville he commanded a superior number of troops, who were rested and well-trained. He drew up a plan to outflank the Confederates as quickly and quietly as possible, famously announcing, "My plan is perfect. May God have mercy on General Lee, for I will have none." Hooker had not bargained for Lee's ability to improvise; he split the Confederate forces and outflanked the Unionists, defeating Hooker's army before it could even begin its task.

Rallying Cry

Many of the generals of the American Civil War were ill suited to their responsibilities, others were wildly eccentric and some, like General John Sedgewick were simply unlucky. Sedgewick was leading Confederate troops at the battle of the Wilderness in 1864. A brave man, who believed in leading by example, he rode out to rally his men in the face of weakening Union resistance, "Come on men!" he shouted. "They couldn't hit an elephant at this dis..." Sadly, they were the last words he uttered.

Old Birdy Ewell

Confederate general Richard S. Ewell, known by his troops as "Old Baldy," was a lisping, beaky-nosed soldier with a habit of cocking his head on one side. Sources differ about whether Ewell believed that he was a bird—he occasionally pecked at his food and made chirping noises—or whether these habits and his personal appearance meant that he was simply compared with a bird. Whatever the truth, it was not helped by the fact that he ate nothing but wheat boiled in milk and muttered to himself, which led to questions about his mental state.

strange habits

Thomas "Stonewall" Jackson was one of the outstanding Confederate generals, but he was also utterly eccentric. Devoutly religious, he refused to fight on Sundays and it was said that "he lives by the New Testament and fights by the Old." He refused to eat pepper, often sucked on lemons, and always ate standing up in order to keep his alimentary canal straight to improve his digestion. At military college his strange behavior earned him the nickname "Fool Tom" Jackson; as a junior officer he had once worn his winter greatcoat throughout a hot summer because he had received no orders to change it.

hand it over

President Abraham Lincoln (1809–1865) was constantly beset by the difficulty of finding suitable generals to lead the Union armies. He was forced to dismiss the overly cautious George McClellan by sending him a telegram that read: "If you don't want to use the army, I should like to borrow it for a while. Yours respectfully, Abraham Lincoln."

Old Sideburns

Ambrose Burnside succeeded McClellan, despite the general's pleas that he was not competent to do the job. Sadly, Burnside was right and after the disastrous battle of Fredericksburg resulted in 15,000 Union casualties, Lincoln removed him from command, remarking "Only Burnside could have managed such a coup, wringing one last spectacular defeat from the jaws of victory." Burnside's impressive facial whiskers meant he was nicknamed "Old Sideburns," and the name has lingered on rather longer than the general's military reputation. Lincoln finally settled on General Ulysses S. Grant for the top job, saying almost gratefully, "I can't spare this man. He fights!"

don't lose your head

Ulysses S. Grant (1822–1885), one of the finest Civil War generals, was a career soldier in the 1840s, but resigned his commission in 1854 to take up farming. The venture was a failure and he joined his father and brother in their leather goods business. On the outbreak of

history bites

war, Grant joined the Union forces and obtained the rank of brigadier-general through the influence of a family friend. On hearing this news, and no doubt recalling his son's earlier professional failures, Grant's father said, "Be careful Ulysses, you are a general now. It's a good job, don't lose it!"

break it up

Every army in the world makes its soldiers break step from a rhythmic march when they cross bridges. In 1850, 226 soldiers lost their lives while crossing the River Maine at Angers France. As they were marching across the ridge, the rhythm of their steps set up a strong resonance on the bridge, creating vibrations strong enough to snap the cables, destroying the bridge, and plunging the soldiers to their deaths.

custer's last stand

George Armstrong Custer (1839–1876) is one of the most famous generals of history and is remembered for his "heroic" last stand at Little Big Horn in 1876. Custer was an instinctive fighter, but not a tactician. He had graduated 34th out of 34 in his West Point class; he was court-martialed in 1867 for disobeying orders, but redeemed himself the following year by massacring 103 innocent Cheyenne, earning himself the nickname, "Squaw-Killer." His performance at Little Big Horn was not heroic, but downright stupid. Desperate to show off his own personal valor, he ignored the advice of his scouts by lighting fires that gave away the position of his force, and when he saw a body of Indians riding away, Custer assumed, against advice, that his enemy were leaving in a panic. Surrounded and outnumbered by the Sioux Indians, the whole of Custer's force was wiped out. Only one horse survived.

The Shortest War

The shortest war in history was fought between Britain and Zanzibar at 9 am on August 27, 1896. Fearful that the new Sultan of Zanzibar would promote German interests over their own, the British ordered the sultan to vacate the throne. He declined and British warships shelled the royal palace. With only one 17th-century canon to defend himself, the sultan surrendered 45 minutes later. In a less than tactful gesture, the British tried to force local residents to pay for the destruction of the palace.

For the record, the longest continuous war in history was probably the 30 Years War, 1618–1648. The 100 Years War was fought intermittently over the course of 114 years between England and France, 1337–1453.

history bites

adopting camouflage

By the beginning of the 20th century, it had become clear that the traditional decorative uniforms worn by the soldiers of almost every "civilized" country looked good on the parade ground but were impractical on the field of battle. Colonial wars in Africa and India against well-camouflaged opponents had taught the British the value of khaki clothing. Of the major combatants in 1914, it was only the French who insisted on sticking to uniforms of red kepis, red trousers, and blue jackets. When one colonel suggested to Marshal Joffre in 1914 that protective steel helmets might be useful in the conflagration, Joffre replied, "My friend, we shall not have time to make them. I shall tear up the Boches within two months."

water, water, everywhere

Napoleon famously declared that "An army marches on its stomach," but soldiers and sailors have always complained about their rations—often with good cause. In the 1870s, the British Navy was still using meat preserved in 1805, the year of Trafalgar. The real problem was a supply of fresh water on ships that were at sea for long periods. In 1845 the warship HMS *America* was becalmed off the South American coast for 97 days. Men were flogged for drinking the captain's bath water and others were forced to drink seawater laced with vinegar. When given command of the *America* the martinet ship's captain, the Hon. John Gordon had not actually been to sea for 27 years and probably owed his appointment to his connections in the government.

Battle of Nerves

The first day of the battle of the Somme in 1916 was one of the bloodiest days in the history of warfare. Allied troops were launched at entrenched German positions along a 25-mile front, believing that a week-long artillery bombardment would have seriously weakened the German ability to respond to a massed infantry attack. British troops were told by a confident leadership, "You will be able to go over the top with a walking stick. You will not need rifles." What the military high command had not realized, however, was that the German troops had sheltered underground in bomb-proof shelters during the artillery barrage. When the infantry attack was launched on July 1, 1916, the Germans emerged to man the machine guns and mow down 60,000 troops in a single day.

In 1903 Douglas Haig, later the architect of the Somme Offensive wrote, "We must never forget that we are dealing with men of flesh and blood and nerves,"—although he seems to have forgotten those words in 1916.

history bites

Simply not Sporting

It may be a peculiarly British trait, but there are many instances of crass comments by military men who intended to launch their troops and weapons at an apparently inferior enemy, only to have their bombastic words shot down in flames shortly afterward.

During the Boer War, General Kitchener only slowly realized that the Boers fought very differently from the Sudanese, his enemy during the 1890s. Instead of fighting from rigid formations like the British, the Boers took cover behind rocks and trees, which the British officers regarded as very poor form. "The Boers are not like the Sudanese who stood up to a fair fight," he wrote in 1900. "They are always running away on their little ponies."

In 1914, when faced by the crack new German naval weapon of submarines, the Comptroller of the Admiralty harrumphed, "Underwater weapons? I call them underhand, unfair, and un-English. They'll never be any use in war and I'll tell you why—I'm going to get the First Sea Lord to announce that we intend to treat all submarines as pirate vessels in wartime. We'll hang their crews." What he seemed to forget was that the Germans were not only utterly un-English, but at the time completely anti-English and used their U-boats with exceptional skill.

military mayhem

underwater combat

During World War I, the British rather belatedly woke up to the need for submarines to combat the German U-boat menace. The K Class submarines were designed to be fast enough on the surface to keep up with a battle fleet in action. Larger and more powerful than any of their predecessors, they were steam-powered and should have been able to wreak havoc on a German fleet. Unfortunately, the reality was rather different. Their very size meant that maneuvering was tricky and on one occasion a captain telephoned his lieutenant with "I say, Number One, my end is diving what's your end up to?" Only 18 were ever built, and of those, four were sunk in accidents. Only one ever fired a torpedo in action.

stuffed shirt

Douglas MacArthur (1880–1964) was a famously autocratic general and infuriated many of those he worked with, not least the president Harry Truman. Truman confided in his diary, "He's worse than the Cabots and Lodges—they at least talked to one another before they told God what to do. Mc tells God right off. It is a very great pity we have to have Stuffed Shirts like that in key positions."

history bites

heady ambition

General Bernard Montgomery (1887–1976) was a gifted commander, but he also demonstrated autocratic tendencies. The chief of the Imperial Staff, General Alanbrook remarked to King George VI that Montgomery was "a very good soldier, but I think he is after my job." "I thought he was after mine!" the king replied.

Winston Churchill later said that Montgomery was "in defeat unbeatable; in victory unbearable."

back tracking

After D-Day and the break-out from Normandy in 1944, the Allies made steady progress across Europe, forcing the Germans to retreat. On some occasions the armies advanced so quickly, they outstripped their supply lines, and indeed exceeded the expectations of the military planners. General Patton received orders to by-pass the city of Triers as it would apparently take four divisions to capture it. By the time he received the message, however, he had already captured the city and was moving on. He sent a prompt reply: "Have taken Triers with two division. Do you want me to give it back?"

Military Mayhem

Pulling Rank

The winter that George Washington's troops spent at Valley Forge in 1777 was the nadir for the Revolutionary Army. "An army of skeletons appeared before our eyes naked, starved, sick and discouraged," wrote New York's Gouverneur Morris to the Continental Congress. Colonel Aaron Burr had tried to improve conditions for his men by providing new shoes and arranging visits from prostitutes. But, defeated and exhausted, some of the troops in the Continental Army threatened to mutiny. As Burr passed down an inspection line, a mutineer aimed a gun at him and pulled the trigger. The gun did not go off as Burr had removed the men's musket cartridges during the night. As the soldier stared in horror and bewilderment, Burr drew his sword and amputated the man's arm with a single stroke. No one questioned his authority again.

Last Chance

At the end of the Civil War, the Confederate president Jefferson Davis (1808–1889) was arrested by Union troops and indicted for treason in 1866. Many northerners were keen to see him executed, but the group who campaigned most vociferously for his freedom was the former slaves from his plantation in Mississippi. After two years' imprisonment, Davis somehow avoided trial and was released.

beastly manners

Although many of the Civil War commanders undoubtedly exhibited the courtly good manners of officers and gentleman, Union General Benjamin Butler (1818–1893) was not one of them. After a few women had jeered at Union troops who were occupying New Orleans in 1862, Butler decreed that any woman who verbally abused his troops "shall be regarded and shall be held liable to be treated as a woman of the town [a prostitute] plying her avocation." The boorish Butler was immediately nicknamed "the beast" and furious women turned their back on him whenever he passed by.

too many chiefs

The invasion of Normandy on D-Day, 1944, began with the nighttime airdrop of troops from the U.S. 82nd and 101st Airborne Divisions. Although casualties were light, the troops were so widely scattered that in many cases it took several days for units to re-form. As a result of this, for the remainder of the war all further Allied airborne operations were conducted in daylight. Many of the infantry units were not so lucky and suffered high casualties, especially among enlisted men. The ratio of officers to men was (temporarily) an incredible 5:1. "Never in the history of human combat have so few been led by so many," remarked General Maxwell Taylor dryly.

discoveries and inventions

sending secret messages

The ability to send secret messages to one's allies that could not be intercepted and read by the enemy has long occupied the minds of military and political planners. Invisible ink and hidden writing are now more often the preserve of children playing spies, but an Arab treatise mentions a recipe as early as 1412. The Greek historian Herodotus records that in 312 BC Histaeus of Miletus shaved the head of a slave, tattooed a message on to his head, and after the hair had grown back, sent the slave off to his destination where the man's head was shaved so that the message could be read. It was not exactly an instant messaging service, but it was at least discreet.

a lot of hot air

Man spent centuries trying to discover the secret of flight and history is littered with the wreckage of many unlikely flying machines. The first people to achieve any sort of success were the French Montgolfier brothers, Joseph and Jacques, from Lyons in southwest

France. The Montgolfier brothers hot air balloon invention attracted much publicity and in 1783 they were invited to demonstrate their balloon before Louis XVI and Marie-Antoinette. Contemporaries were quick to see the potential of hot air balloons, but the Montgolfiers remained cautious. Only one of the brothers (Joseph) ever flew in a balloon, and it was an experience he did not care to repeat.

birth of the fork

Catherine de Medici (1519–1589) was credited with many wicked things by her enemies in France, but she was also responsible for introducing the fork to polite French society after her marriage to the King Henri II in 1533. Forks were slow to catch on as many people regarded their use as an affectation, and in England, people asked "Why should a person need a fork when God had given him hands?" Gradually, however, the use of forks became fashionable among the wealthy, and they evolved from two tines to four as it became clear that they were more efficient eating utensils than simple knives. Prior to the introduction of the fork, people generally carried their own cutlery, usually a sharply pointed knife, which was used to spear the food and raise it to the mouth; these knives could also be used as weapons and there are innumerable accounts of violence around the dining tables of Europe. As the fork became more widely accepted, the need for pointed knives declined and in 1669 Louis XIV of France declared that pointed knives were illegal and had all the knives of Versailles ground down in order to reduce dinner table fights.

a fine nose

In the late 16th-century, revelations in the world of astronomy had to fit in with the Church's view of heaven and earth and passions clearly ran high between rival scientists. The Danish astronomer Tycho Brahe (1546–1601) lost his whole nose after a duel in 1565 that was fought over a mathematical argument. Brahe not only survived the encounter, but also made a rather fine prosthetic nose from gold, silver, and wax, which he wore for the rest of his life.

keeping it sweet

The flushing lavatory was invented by Queen Elizabeth I's godson Sir John Harrington, who showcased his invention in a pamphlet entitled *The Metamorphosis of Ajax*, a subtle pun on "jakes," the Elizabethan word for lavatory. Harrington urged his readers to find a "way to cleanse and keep sweete the noblest parte of themselves." The Queen was so impressed that she ordered one to be built at Richmond Palace in 1598, but it was not until 250 years later in 1848 that a Victorian Public Health Act decreed that every new house should be equipped with a "wc, privy, or ash pit."

history bites

bringing a little sparkle

Champagne has always been considered a drink for special occasions (although the 18th-century dandy Beau Brummel used to polish his shoes with it), but it is ironic given its associations with celebrations and partying that it should have been discovered by a monk. Dom Perignon was a Benedictine monk who was appointed cellarmaster at the Abbey of Hautvillers in 1668. He was the first to successfully blend grapes and contain the sparkling wine in glass bottles by sealing them with Spanish corks. Most people are delighted by the initial sensation of champagne on their tongues, but Don Perignon's reaction was more lyrical than most: "Brothers," he said, "Come quickly! I am drinking stars!"

raven protection

Charles II (1630–1685) was a great patron of science and learning and funded, among other things, the construction of a new royal observatory at Greenwich. While it was being built in 1675, the Astronomer Royal, Sir John Flamsteed, took up residence at the Tower of London where his observations were frequently disturbed by the ravens. The king was on the point of ordering the destruction of the birds when Flamsteed stopped him and reminded His Majesty of the superstition associated with them. If the ravens leave the

Tower, it is a sign that the kingdom is about to fall. As Flamsteed pointed out, Charles had only recently repossessed his throne and it would be a shame to lose it again so soon.

the end is nigh

Sir Isaac Newton (1642–1727) was, without doubt, one of the greatest scientists in history. He is famous for the development of calculus, for formulating the law of gravitation, for his studies into the nature of light, and for work that led to the construction of the first telescope. He was always modest about his achievements and how they came about, famously writing, "If I have seen further than others it is by standing on the shoulders of giants." He penned these words in a letter to his rival and critic Robert Hooke, another noted scientist, but a man of short stature. Could Newton have been poking fun at his critic?

Newton spent part of his career dabbling in alchemy and wrote a remarkable study on the Apocalypse, which included an attempt to decode the Bible, that Newton believed contained God's secret laws for the universe. He predicted that the most likely date for the Apocalypse was 2060.

history bites

the cost of horse power

Many inventors and engineers make lousy businessmen, but James
Watt (1736–1819) was not one of them. In 1755 he had patented his
steam engine design and in 1773 went into business with Matthew
Boulton, whose Birmingham factory produced Watt's engines and
sold them to mine owners. Watt charged his customers high prices
for his engines; he compared his machines to horses and worked out
how much money his customers saved by using his machine rather
than a team of horses. Instead of paying a flat price for the engine,
customers agreed to pay one third of the amount saved to Watt every
year for an incredible 25 years.

Puffing devil

The engineer Richard Trevithick (1771–1833) was a tall man known
in his youth for his immense strength that was manifested in his
ability to throw sledgehammers over the rooftops of engine houses.
However, while working with his father at the Ding Dong mine in
Cornwall, Trevithick became interested in engineering and the
application of steam power. In 1801, he designed a steam-powered
car known as the "Puffing Devil," which conveyed Trevithick and
three delighted friends half a mile up Camborne Hill. The vehicle was
destroyed when it ran off the road and crashed into a house. One

eyewitness reported that rather than clearing up the mess, "the parties adjourned to the Hotel and comforted their hearts with Roast Goose and proper drinks when, forgetful of the Engine, its water boiled away, the iron became red hot and nothing that was combustible remained either of the engine or the house."

too shy

Henry Cavendish (1731–1810) was one of the brightest scientific minds of the 18th century, but he was a man so crippled by shyness that he hated virtually all social contact and communicated with his servants via handwritten notes. He enjoyed attending meetings at the Royal Society, but could rarely bring himself to actually speak to his colleagues. Extremely rich, he set up a magnificent laboratory in his house in Clapham, but he was so shy about his work that it was not until long after his death that researchers discovered the extent of his knowledge. His contemporaries were often astonished by his allusions to experiments they had not even heard of, but Cavendish is credited with being the first person to correctly assess the mass of the earth, an exacting calculation and an amazing experiment to organize in the latter half of the 18th century that took more than a year to complete.

history bites

getting lost

In 1707, one of the Royal Navy's finest commanders, the wonderfully named Sir Cloudsley Shovell, perished off the Scilly Isles with all hands as his ship *Association* ran aground—thanks not to bad weather or enemy action, but because of a navigational error. Before the end of the 18th century, sailors had no accurate means of measuring longitude and depended on the very inaccurate method of "dead reckoning." After the loss of Shovell's ship in 1714, the government announced the award of £20,000 ($35,000) to anyone who could produce an accurate marine chronometer. After some 40 years' work, John Harrison's fourth attempt was recognized to have solved the problem in 1765 by the exacting (and mean-minded) Board of Longitude. Incredibly, given the critical nature of this instrument to maritime safety, the navy then wavered over whether to issue it to all ships of the line. Budgetary considerations then, as now, were a problem as each chronometer cost an incredible £500 ($800) to make; to put this in perspective, when the ship HMS *Bounty* was purchased it cost £1,800 ($3,500).

no latin, no membership

Edward Jenner (1749–1823), the country doctor who had pioneered the use of vaccination against smallpox in 1796, was proposed for membership of the Royal College of Physicians in London in 1813. His membership was turned down not because the college felt that his medical qualifications were deficient, but because he lacked the necessary knowledge of classical languages and texts then deemed necessary for entry to professional institutions.

mice on toast, anyone?

The Reverend William Buckland (1784–1856) was a leading geologist and authority on fossilized remains. He was one of the first people to identify dinosaur remains, but despite his great learning, he is almost as famous for his eccentricities. A true gourmand, he was keen to eat his way through the animal kingdom and was generous in his hospitality. Guests were never sure what to expect at his table and the writer John Ruskin regretted that he was not present for a meal of mice on toast. Buckland relished almost everything he ate, except moles, which he said were disgusting.

man of steam

The engineer George Stephenson (1781–1848) did not learn to read and write until he was 18, but he gained a great knowledge of practical engineering by dismantling and reassembling engines at Killingworth Colliery where he worked. By 1812, when he was 41, he was employed as the colliery's engine wright. He was well aware of the dangers of working down a mine, particularly of the problems associated with poisonous gases and in 1815 he developed a lamp that could be used safely underground. Unfortunately, the noted scientist Sir Humphrey Davy had produced a similar item around about the same time, and he was a man with far better connections than a mere colliery man. Davy wrote sneeringly that he could not understand how Stephenson, "a person not even possessing a knowledge of the elements of chemistry" managed it.

Stephenson, of course, went on to build Britain's first railway. He was an engineer of genius, but his humble background did not help him in the fight to convince the vested interests of landowners that the railways were the way forward for Britain's future. One opponent riposted, "This railway is the most absurd scheme that ever entered into the head of a man to conceive. Mr Stephenson never had a plan —I do not believe he is capable of making one..."

moving about

The Duke of Wellington was another opponent of railway travel, noting sardonically that, "it will only encourage the lower classes to move about." Wellington later changed his mind, however, perhaps helped by the fact that the railway entrepreneur George Hudson (known as the "Railway King") had convinced him to invest in the schemes that produced a tidy profit.

Faster than the speed of...

Thomas Carlyle described a journey on the Liverpool to Manchester railway in 1842: "I was most dreadfully frightened before the train started; in the nervous state I was in, it seemed to me certain that I should faint, from the impossibility of getting the horrid thing stopped."

The train was probably traveling at a speed of 25 mph, about twice as fast as a stagecoach. When the railway opened in 1830, contemporaries were dazzled by the speed of travel. The first railway casualty was the cabinet minister William Huskisson, who, "less active from the effects of age and ill-health, bewildered, too, by the frantic cries of 'Stop the engine! Clear the track!' that resonated on all sides, completely lost his head, looked helplessly to the right and left, and was instantaneously prostrated by that fatal machine..."

head rolling

Richard Owen (1804–1892) was one of the great paleontologists of the 19th century. He was the man responsible for naming dinosaurs and later in his career established the Natural History Museum in

London, fighting against the odds to make it a place accessible to ordinary people rather than just scientists and academics. Owen trained as a doctor and was fascinated by anatomy to the extent that he sometimes borrowed limbs and body parts from the local morgue to study at home. One evening, while carrying home the head of an African sailor in a sack, Owen slipped on a cobble and watched in horror as the head rolled out of the sack and passed through the open door of a cottage, coming to rest in the front room, to the consternation of the occupants.

Finding a bride

Charles Darwin (1809–1882) was a meticulous naturalist and the originator of the theory of evolution via natural selection. From his personal papers it is clear that he applied the same rigorously scientific tests to personal decisions as he did to his work. In 1838, probably under pressure from his father to find a wife, he drew up a list of pros and cons for marriage. Under the list of negatives he bleakly noted the "loss of time—cannot read in the evenings—fatness and idleness—anxiety and responsibility—less money for books, etc." At the end of the pros, having remarked, "One cannot live this solitary life... friendless and cold, and childless" he wrote briskly, "Never mind, trust to chance—Keep a sharp look out—There is many a happy slave." Darwin married his cousin Emma Wedgwood the following year.

not up to scratch

The history of science and discovery is littered with tales of petty rivalries and strange ambitions. The American paleontologist Edwin Drinker Cope spent a large part of his career in bitter dispute with his one-time partner Othniel Charles Marsh, as they competed to unveil fossils across America. Cope's final ambition was for his skeleton to become the type specimen for *Homo Sapiens*, a privilege normally reserved for the first set of bones discovered for a particular species. As no one else had laid down a human type specimen, Cope willed his bones to the Wistar Institute, who discovered during the preparation of the skeleton that it showed signs of syphilis, an unfortunate attribute for the type bones of the human species.

sewing nightmare

Elias Howe (1819–1867) came up with the ingenious mechanics of the sewing machine after a dream in which he dreamed he was being attacked by ferocious natives with spears. Initially, he never made much money from his idea, although he patented it in 1846. He returned from an unsuccessful tour of England, where he had tried to interest the great cotton mills in the idea, to discover that Isaac Singer had infringed his patent by adapting Howe's ideas for his single-thread chain-stitch sewing machine. After seven years of litigation, Howe's rights were recognized and Singer was forced to pay him compensation. Although Howe finally amassed a fortune, Singer's name is the one that is remembered by posterity.

bright spark

Michael Faraday (1791–1867) was one of the most distinguished scientists of the Victorian era. The son of a London blacksmith, he was initially apprenticed to a bookbinder but his attendance at a lecture given by Sir Humphrey Davy in 1812 proved to be a life-changing event. He became Davy's assistant and gained an invaluable scientific education. His greatest life's work was his *Experimental Researches in Electricity,* which broadened contemporary knowledge considerably. He is regarded as one of the greatest experimental physicists in history, and usually succeeded in explaining to laymen how his discoveries could be put to a wider use. When Gladstone asked him about the practical use of one particular discovery, Faraday replied, "Why sir, there is the probability that you will soon be able to tax it."

discoveries and inventions

the height of pens

The story of the ballpoint pen echoes that of the sewing machine, in that the inventor and man who took out the original patent failed to exploit the commercial advantages of the product. Laszlo Biro and his brother Georg are credited with the invention of the ballpoint pen in 1938 (now universally known as the "Biro"), but in fact the first ballpoint was patented in 1888 by John J. Loud, who invented a pen for marking leather. Loud's pen had a more limited use than that dreamed up by Biro 50 years later. Biro was a journalist who wanted to create a pen that used quick-drying ink to minimize smudges. He noticed that printer's ink dried fast, leaving the paper dry, but it was a far thicker liquid than conventional ink used in fountain pens, so Biro devised a new tip for the pen—a tiny ball-bearing which rotated and picked up ink from the cartridge. During World War II, the British government purchased the licensing rights to the Biro so that they could supply fighter pilots with pens that would not leak under pressure.

suitable ink

The matter of suitable ink has plagued writers and printers since the earliest times. Johann Gutenberg, the creator of the first mechanical printing press in 1452, created a mixture from linseed oil and soot, which would not fade or smudge the type by being too thick. His very first press was constructed from a wine press—a screw-type device that enabled him to squeeze water out of the damp paper when it emerged from the press.

great foresight

Benjamin Franklin is credited with the invention of many things, among them bifocal spectacles. Like many middle-aged people today, Franklin had two pairs of glasses, one pair for reading and the other for distance viewing. Tired with continually swapping them over he decided to merge them: "I had the glasses cut, and half of each kind associated in the same circle. By this means, as I wear my spectacles constantly, I have only to move my eyes up or down, as I want to see distinctly far or near, the proper glasses being always ready."

novelty telephones

Although today the USA boasts more telephones per head of population than any nation on earth, when Alexander Graham Bell (1847–1922) demonstrated his "electrical speaking telephone" to the executives of the Western Union in 1876, he was dismissed with a polite letter: "After careful consideration of your invention, while it is a very interesting novelty, we have come to the conclusion that it has no economical possibilities." Fortunately, Bell found more far-sighted investors and by the turn of the century there were over six million telephones in America.

The introduction and widespread use of the telephone penetrated the whole of society and introduced new words and phrases into the language, such as "I'll give you a ring."

The eccentric baronet Sir George Sitwell (1860–1943)—a man who was more predisposed to writing learned treatises on the history of the fork than adapting to new-fangled appliances—complained to his son Osbert that someone had promised to give him a ring, but the expected item of jewelry had never arrived. "Such a pity to promise people things and then forget about them," he grumbled.

WORK ethic

Thomas Edison (1847–1931), one of the most prolific and successful inventors of the 19th and early 20th centuries, was expelled from school for being retarded. He surmounted this initial setback by working extremely hard and is well known for saying that "Genius is one percent inspiration and 99 percent perspiration." He worked his staff equally hard, and his assistants were referred to as the "insomnia squad" by the rest of his employees.

history bites

In the 1920s, Edison teamed up with Henry Ford and Ford moved the great inventor's original laboratory from Menlo Park, New Jersey, to his museum in Dearborn, Michigan. Everything was meticulously laid out as it had been and the new building was opened in 1929. Ford asked Edison what he thought of it. "It's 99 and half percent perfect," replied Edison. Ford was alarmed. "What's wrong?" he asked."Well, we never used to keep the place so clean!" Edison replied.

Henry Ford obviously regarded Edison as something of a hero, as he bottled his dying breath and it remains on display at the Ford Museum in Michigan.

Edison himself was well aware of his fame and the importance of his work to history. It was suggested when he died that the world should observe two minutes without electricity, but it proved impossible to execute this act of recognition.

Tributes like this did occur in the US though. In 1922, when Alexander Graham Bell died, the phones of America fell silent for a minute to mark his funeral, and when Marconi died a few years later in 1937, two minutes radio silence was observed throughout the world.

discoveries and inventions

ivory substitute

It is hard to imagine a world without plastic, but it was not invented until 1869 and did not enter widespread use in its present form until the 1950s. In 1869, a billiard ball manufacturer offered a $10,000 prize to anyone who could find a suitable material from which to fashion billiard balls. Before 1869 the balls were made of ivory, which was extremely costly and increasingly rare. The competition was won by Isaiah and John Wesley Hyatt, who produced celluloid, the forerunner of plastic. John Hyatt (1837–1920) was an accomplished inventor, who had already manufactured a knife sharpener, a multiple-needle sewing machine, and the Hyatt roller bearing. Celluloid was his most successful creation and was achieved by mixing camphor with cellulose nitrate; it was used not only for billiard balls, but also in dominoes.

The English chemist and inventor Alexander Parkes (1812–1890) had already toyed with celluloid and had patented an early form, xylonite, in 1855. Noted for his experiments in electroplating (he even electroplated a spider's web), Parkes was another boffin who failed to make a commercial success of his work.

history bites

too many patents

In 1899, Charles Duell resigned from his job as head of the U. S. Patent office, possibly worn out by the proliferation of inventions that crossed his desk every day. He declared that, "Everything that can be invented has been invented."

impossible ship designs

The history of naval design is littered with ships which should have been wrecked before they were launched, none more so than the incredible circular ships designed by the Russian Admiral Popov in the 1870s. Popov intended to build a stable platform for large caliber guns that could guard the shallow waters of the Black Sea and then steam off if required elsewhere. Three ships were laid down, the *Popov*, *Novogorod,* and the yacht *Livadia*, the last of which was intended as a royal yacht for Tsar Alexander II. As stable platforms, the gunships were reasonably efficient, but their shape meant that they were impossible to sail: it was terribly difficult to steer anything approaching a straight course, and when caught in a current the ships simply spun around in circles. Making the best of a bad (and expensive) job, *Popov* and *Novorogod* were designated Coastal Defense Armor Clad ships in 1892 and were used as store ships from 1903 until they were scrapped in 1913.

discoveries and inventions

radioactive material

Marie Curie worked for over 30 years to research the nature of the strange force she had named "radioactivity." Marie won two Nobel prizes and helped found the prestigious Radium Institute at the University of Paris, but her work eventually killed her. She had no idea that the long-term effects of the radiation that so fascinated her were lethal, and she died of leukaemia in 1934. She made some of the most important scientific advances of the 20th century, but her papers and books, now stored in lead-lined boxes, are virtually inaccessible today because they remain contaminated by radioactivity.

computer maniac

John von Neumann (1903–1957) was a Hungarian-born American mathematician and pioneer in the field of computers. During World War II, he succeeded in designing the first "electronic brain" for the U.S. government. He called it a "Mathematical Analyzer, Numerical Integrator, and Computer." In a period obsessed with abbreviations and acronyms, it was some days before colleagues realized that the shortened form was MANIAC.

history bites

Neumann clearly possessed a dry wit. He declared in 1949, "It would appear we have reached the limits of what it is possible to achieve with computer technology, although we should be careful with such statements—they tend to sound pretty silly in five years."

tv addict

Television was invented by the Scotsman John Logie Baird (1888–1946), a remarkable man and a talented electrical engineer. He filed a patent for a "televisor" design in 1923 and the following year demonstrated broadcast images. Laird approached the British Broadcasting Corporation (BBC) to try to interest them in beginning commercial television broadcasts, but despite the obvious advantages of Baird's system, the BBC adopted the rival Marconi-EMI technology in 1937.

The reason for this was that the director-general John Reith had attended the Royal Technical College in Glasgow with Laird in 1906. An autocratic bully, Reith was withdrawn from the college only after he had fallen out with Baird, and 25 years later, he evidently still harbored a grudge.

discoveries and inventions

dropping the bomb

Robert Oppenheimer (1904–1967) watched the explosion of the first atomic bomb at the New Mexico test site with mixed feelings, only too aware of the implications of his work. He later wrote that a line from the Hindu holy scripture the *Bhagavad Gita* went through his head, "I am become Death, Destroyer of Worlds." Just three weeks later, a 10,000 lb bomb was dropped on Hiroshima. Years later, the pilot who bombed Hiroshima had a rather less profound reaction than Oppenheimer: "The whole sky is lit up in the prettiest blues and pinks I've ever seen in my life. It was just great!"

a misguided obituary

It is one of the great ironies of history that the man who did so much to improve humankind's ability to blow itself up also endowed the most famous peace prize of the 20th century. Chemist Alfred Nobel (1833–1896) invented dynamite in 1866 and gelignite nine years later; he amassed a huge fortune by creating an industrial empire based on their manufacture. In 1888, he was perturbed to read his own obituary in the newspaper and was further disturbed by the fact that posterity would remember him as the man who invented and disseminated the world's most successful weapons of mass destruction. The obituary should have been for his brother, but it spurred Nobel to endow the monumental awards that bear his name and are awarded annually for peace, chemistry, physics, medicine, literature, and economics. Mathematics was apparently left off the list because a mathematician once had an affair with his wife.

EXPLORERS

SMALL WORLD

The notion of a spherical world must have seemed incredibly strange to people brought up on the idea of a flat earth. Columbus believed that the world was far smaller than it really is and when he reached Cuba, he thought it he had arrived in mainland Japan.

UNKNOWN HEROES

The history of exploration is littered with tales of unknown heroes, whose glory was often snatched by the more famous expedition leaders. Christopher Columbus (1451–1506) amassed fame and fortune for his discovery of the Americas, but after a voyage of ten weeks across the Atlantic Ocean, land was actually sighted by a sailor named Rodrigo Bernajo. Columbus took the credit and named the small island in the Bahamas San Salvador. Despite his momentous contribution, Bernajo seems to have disappeared from history.

Given Columbus's much-publicized discovery of the Americas in 1492, it is perhaps surprising that the continent does not bear his name. It is instead named after Amerigo Vespucci, an Italian who procured ships' supplies in Seville. His connections enabled him to make a couple of journeys to the New World, but only in the capacity of a passenger, rather than as a Conquistador or explorer. The mists of time effectively mask how rumors began about his discovery of the New World, but one German cartographer believed them and endowed the new continent with his name.

Strike it Lucky

In 1497 the Genoese explorer John Cabot (1425–1500) was financed by the merchants of Bristol and King Henry VII, who hoped that Cabot would return from his voyage into the unknown with spices and treasure, and net them a profit. Cabot struck lucky, making landfall only four weeks after leaving Bristol. He claimed the new territories, or "Newfoundland," in the name of Henry VII, and his sailors were amazed by the amount of fish in the waters, so thick "a person could walk across their backs;" they claimed that they were able to catch vast numbers simply by dipping baskets into the water. Cabot thought he had discovered a new island off the coast of China and Henry VII was immediately impressed by his discovery, rewarding him with a princely £10 ($18) for his troubles.

Mapping New Territory

Exploration of the New World undoubtedly exacerbated tensions in the Old, as rival nations vied to find the most lucrative new lands to exploit. Cabot's voyage aroused great interest and initiated a spate of espionage. In December 1497, an English spy, John Day, wrote in Spanish to "the most magnificent and most worthy lord, the lord grand admiral," in Spain. The letter was almost certainly intended for Columbus and Day gives a detailed account of Cabot's voyage and discoveries. He included a map which showed Columbus exactly what Cabot had found, noting that the cape of Newfoundland "is 1800 miles west of Dursey Head which is in Ireland."

Drake's Booty

By the time of the Spanish Armada in 1588 the very name of Sir Francis Drake struck fear into the heart of the average Spanish sailor. Drake (c. 1540–1596) had a well-deserved reputation as the scourge of the Spanish, and had grown extremely wealthy from pursuing and capturing the ships of the Spanish treasure fleets. Despite orders to work together with the rest of the fleet during the English defensive actions of the Armada campaign, Drake could not resist seizing a prize when the opportunity arose. When the Spanish ship *Rosario* came into view during the night of July 31, 1588, Drake pounced, capturing the ship and all its treasure despite the fact that he should have been leading a squadron of the British fleet. What is unclear is why the Spanish captain put up absolutely no resistance to the English attack. Despite the presence of 300 pike men on his ship, he was so overawed that he simply handed it over to Drake, a man he later described as endowed with "valour and felicity so great that Mars and Neptune seemed to attend him." Drake was not only flattered, but also considerably richer.

Royal Potatoes

The Spanish explorer Gonzalo Jiménez de Quesada (c. 1497–1597) first came across a potato in 1537 in South America (although the Anglo-Saxon world attributes its discovery to Sir Walter Raleigh in 1585) and soon discovered that they were easy to grow, could be preserved for a reasonably long time, and were a useful food source when treated properly. Europeans were rather suspicious of potatoes at first, confusing them with the poisonous deadly nightshade plant and suspecting that at the very least potatoes caused flatulence. Potatoes eventually became fashionable when taken up by royalty: Queen Marie-Antoinette wore potato flowers in her hair.

beer rations

All ships left port heavily provisioned, but for those embarking on voyages of exploration, provisioning must have been especially difficult: even the best prepared captain could only have a vague idea of what he would encounter and how long he would be away from home. Fresh water was always a particular problem and even when stored in casks it did not remain fresh for long. Rainwater or melted snows were the only other sources when at sea. Sailors depended on wine or beer, with a ration of one gallon per man per day. Sir Martin Frobisher (1535–1594), the Englishman who set out to explore the North-West Passage in 1576 apparently announced, "We'll sail as long as the beer lasts."

tobacco high

Scholar and scientist Thomas Hariot (1560–1621) accompanied Sir Walter Raleigh on his colonizing voyages to Virginia and published an account of the expedition in which he wrote lyrically about the benefits of tobacco. He described the English copying the Indian habit of crumbling the leaves and smoking them, [we] "used to suck it after their manner, as also since our return have found many rare and wonderful experiments of the virtues thereof, of which the relation would require a volume by itself." Hariot may have become too fond of tobacco: he died of cancer of the nose in 1621.

Patience of an astronomer

The question of how far the sun is from the earth troubled astronomers until the middle of the 18th century. Edmund Halley (1656–1742) realized that it could be calculated from the transit of Venus, that is when the planet Venus passes across the face of the sun, an event which occurs in pairs every 105–120 years. Halley discovered this in 1716, and worked out the next transits would occur in 1761 and 1769; it did not take a degree in mathematics for him to know that he would be dead by then. Undeterred Halley published a detailed plan for the astronomers of the 1760s, which explained that the further apart the observers were on earth, the more accurate the measurements would be. The transit lasts only seven hours, so it was vital for the astronomers to be in the right place at the right time. This was no mean feat as the transit would only be visible from South Africa, Siberia, North America, the Indian Ocean, the South Pacific, and Central America.

By 1760, England was embroiled in the Seven Years War with France, which was conducted across Europe and the colonial holdings in America and India. Travel for an astronomer laden with sensitive instruments would not be easy.

EXPLORERS

Jean Baptiste Chappe d'Auteroche was sent to Tobolsk in Siberia, traveling across the vast country by horse-drawn sled and only just crossing the frozen Volga before the ice broke up. He had to cope with the spring thaw, the "rasputitsa" which turns the frozen earth to impenetrable sludge, and arrived in Tobolsk with only six days to spare. He unpacked his carefully preserved instruments, but had to be protected from the violence of local peasants by a Cossack guard. The spring thaw was unusually severe and the locals believed that the French stranger, with his collection of unusual instruments, was the cause.

Perhaps the most determined, but hapless astronomer was the Frenchman Guillaume Le Gentil, who was sent to Pondicherry in 1760. Prevented from landing by a British siege, he observed the transit of Venus from the heaving deck of his ship and his calculations were pretty much worthless. Undaunted and extremely dedicated, he decided to remain in Mauritius for eight years to await the next transit. In March 1768 he arrived in Pondicherry via a circuitous route, where he received a hero's welcome from the governor and set up an observatory. The weather was perfect until a massive front of clouds arrived the evening before the transit and stubbornly hovered over Pondicherry for the next few days. Having traveled 70,000 miles, spent nine years abroad, and risked his life through war and tropical disease, Le Gentil could observe nothing, and with commendable understatement he wrote in his journal "I was more than two weeks in a singular dejection."

anything for a nail

The remarkable explorer Captain James Cook (1728–1779) arrived in Tahiti in 1769 after many months at sea. Not surprisingly, the sailors were delighted to see dry land and many beautiful semi-naked Tahitian women. Metal objects fascinated the Tahitians, from shiny naval instruments and swords, right down to the very nails that held the ship together and they would do almost anything to possess a nail. The first European vessel to visit Tahiti in 1767, HMS *Dolphin*, nearly fell apart on its departure because the sailors had been removing nails from the body of the ship to present to local women.

Cook knew this and had hidden extra barrels of nails in the hold. He also issued strict orders to his men: "No Iron Tools, Nails large or small, shall be given to the Natives in exchange for anything but Provisions and Refreshments, as it has been found that these are the most valuable articles in their eyes."

kangaroo meat

The noted botanist Sir Joseph Banks (1744–1820) accompanied James Cook on his 1769 expedition. He was the first European to see a kangaroo, an animal quite unlike anything ever seen in Europe. It was "of a mouse-colour and very swift," he noted, not quite being able to believe that so large an animal moved around by hopping. "What to liken him to I cannot tell," he wrote. Three weeks after first sighting the animal called "kangaru" by the local aborigines, Banks shot and ate one, pronouncing it very tasty.

hidden by miscalculation

Captain William Bligh (1754–1817) carried a copy of Harrison's famous marine chronometer on board HMS *Bounty* in 1787 and noted in his log that the mutineers made off with his charts and the precious chronometer, when they cast him and 18 shipmates adrift. They left Bligh without navigational aids, saying, "Damn your eyes, you are well off to get what you have." When Fletcher Christian found Pitcairn Island, he discovered, thanks to the chronometer, that its location was not charted correctly, and it was this cartographic error that confirmed them in their decision to settle on the island. They felt confident that they would never be discovered by the British authorities and would thus escape the certain death that awaited them if brought to justice.

dreams turn to mud

The Scottish explorer of West Africa, Mungo Park (1771–1806) was enthused by a love of the Dark Continent and his great curiosity about the native population. His explorations helped to pinpoint the direction of flow of the Niger River. On his second expedition in 1805, he set out with a team of 45, but they gradually deserted him, until he was alone, dependent on guidance from the local people, many of whom seemed hostile.

Before he disappeared, Park sent back his notebooks, which recount his extraordinary journeys with a dispassionate detachment, which seems almost comic. One of his objectives was to search for the legendary golden town of Tellem and the last entry in his journal read, "Tomorrow, we should reach Tellem, a city that has haunted my dreams since I was a child. I cannot sleep for the excitement." He was probably disappointed when he arrived to find it was a village of mud houses.

camel drunks

The first men to traverse Australia from south to north were Robert Burke (1820–1861) and William Wills (1834–1861), and although they lost their lives in the attempt they are probably the continent's most famous explorers. A former policeman, Burke had absolutely no experience of the Australian bush before he set off, and he departed, against all advice, in the early part of the summer in 1860, when temperatures averaged 90 degrees farenheit. They set off laden with supplies, which included an oak table, 12 dandruff brushes for the camels, and ten pairs of hobble for oxen—although there were no oxen on the expedition. They used camels as pack animals, which proved to be willful and obdurate, often because they were drunk: incredibly the camels were often revived with some of the 60 gallons of rum the expedition carried.

canned expedition

As late as the 19th century, explorers were still trying to find the Northwest Passage, a sea route that links the Pacific and Atlantic oceans via the Arctic. Before the construction of the Panama Canal trading ships had to travel from Europe to the west coast of America via India and China, so sailors were keen to cut the journey time by finding a shorter route. The British explorer Sir John Franklin (1786–1847) made four journeys to the region, where he mapped 1,200 miles of coastline and made geological and scientific records. On his second voyage in 1819–1822, his team ran out of food and were forced to eat the leather part of their clothes.

Franklin nevertheless returned a national hero and when another expedition was proposed in 1845, Franklin was somehow the natural choice for leader, despite the fact that he had been retired for 20 years. Franklin set out with enough food to provision his 129-man crew for three years, but when nothing had been heard from him two years later in 1847, the first of 39 rescue parties was dispatched to find him. It now seems that Franklin and his men did not simply perish from exposure in the frozen wastes of the Arctic, but they may have been poisoned by the lead that sealed their 8,000 cans of food.

the blessings of a good thick skirt

A remarkable woman, Mary Kingsley (1862–1900) embarked on exploring West Africa in 1893 after nursing her parents for many years. She recorded her travels in two volumes of witty memoirs that recorded her valuable scientific fieldwork as well as her adventures. She was very much a product of her age and naturally wore the voluminous skirts that were the lot of Victorian women.

Today, they may not appear to be the most practical garb for jungle exploration in the tropics, but Kingsley fiercely denied ever wearing trousers. "As for encasing the more earthward extremities of my anatomy in trousers," she wrote, "I would rather have perished on a scaffold!"

She once fell 15 feet into a stake-lined animal trap in the jungle but was saved from serious injury or even death by the voluminous folds of her clothes. As she wryly noted, "It is at these times you realise the blessings of a good thick skirt... Had I paid heed to the advice of many people in England... and adopted masculine garments, I should have been spiked to the bone and done for."

ROUGH TRAVELS

Sir Richard Burton (1821–1890) was one of the most remarkable Victorian explorers, who traveled across Arabia, Africa, and South America. He was a charismatic man, who, from an early age suffered from impatience and became known as "Ruffian Dick" for his habit of challenging his schoolmates to duels. Rebelling against his parents' efforts to make him learn the violin, the young Burton smashed the violin over the head of his teacher.

Enormously erudite, Burton could speak 40 languages, some so fluently that he could pass as a native. He was driven by a ceaseless urge to discover unknown lands and understand the customs of the native peoples, but he did it all with the careless authority and bravery of an empire-builder. In 1857, accompanied by John Hanning Speke, he set out to discover the source of the Nile and journeyed uncomfortably through East Africa.

history bites

The conditions they experienced would have deterred lesser men, but they were undaunted by malarial swamps, killer bees, or the ravages of smallpox. When they finally arrived at Lake Tanganyika, Speke was almost blind and Burton was (temporarily) paralyzed by malarial fever, in his words "so feeble that we could hardly sit our asses."

building the suez canal

The role of diplomats and engineers is often overlooked in the job of opening up the world to travel. The Frenchman Ferdinand de Lesseps (1805–1894) was responsible for the construction of the two great canals that changed the face of circumnavigation in the 19th century. De Lesseps was a diplomat and land agent, not an engineer, but he used his formidable charm to persuade the many interested parties to overcome their conflicting ambitions to build the Suez Canal.

The British had invested a great deal of energy in an overland railway route across Suez, and the great railway engineer George Stephenson uncharitably damned Lessep's proposal as a "great stinking ditch."

De Lesseps went on to supervise the construction of the Panama Canal, an idea that had first been suggested by the Conquistador Hernan Cortez in the 16th century. At that time, the Holy Roman

Emperor Charles V put an end to the plans, saying, "What God has joined, let no man put asunder."

Situations Vacant

One hundred years ago, polar exploration was regarded as one of the final frontiers of exploration on Earth, but it was not a job for the faint-hearted. When Ernest Shackleton (1874–1922) was recruiting for his 1914 expedition to be the first to cross Antarctica from sea to sea, he simply put an ad in the newspaper:

"Men wanted for hazardous journey. Small wages, bitter cold. Long months of complete darkness. Constant danger, safe return doubtful. Honour and recognition in case of success."

Out of 5,000 applicants, Shackleton picked 28 men. They went on to endure untold privations as natural forces combined to stymie their expedition at every turn: their ship, *Endurance*, was crushed in the ice and eventually Shackleton and five companions had to make a treacherous journey across 800 miles of the south Atlantic in a lifeboat to South Georgia to raise a rescue party. Despite all this, not one man died.

history bites

camel water

Wilfred Thesiger (1910–2003) explored the most remote and inhospitable parts of Arabia. He crossed the Empty Quarter twice, something few Europeans contemplated yet alone achieved. One essential piece of advice he passed on to was to avoid drinking water that the camels had passed water in.

acknowledgments

Thanks to Clare Haworth-Maden and Jonathan Millidge for their help and advice, and the usual suspects who suggested quirky historical stories for this book.

Every attempt has been made by the publisher to secure the appropriate permissions for material reproduced in this book. If there has been any oversight we will be happy to rectify the situation and written submission should be made to the publishers.